Best Canadian Essays
2013

Best Canadian Essays
2013

Edited by Christopher Doda
and Stephen Marche

TIGHTROPE BOOKS

Tightrope Books
167 Browning Trail
Barrie, Ontario. L4N 5E7
www.tightropebooks.com

Series editor: Christopher Doda
Guest editor: Stephen Marche
Cover design: Deanna Janovski
Book design and typography: Dawn Kresan

We thank the Canada Council for the Arts and the Ontario Arts
Council for their support of our publishing program.

Canada Council   Conseil des Arts
for the Arts   du Canada

ONTARIO ARTS COUNCIL
CONSEIL DES ARTS DE L'ONTARIO

PRINTED AND BOUND IN CANADA

A CATALOGUING RECORD FOR THIS PUBLICATION
IS AVAILABLE FROM LIBRARY AND ARCHIVES CANADA

CONTENTS

Prologue

This volume marks the fifth anniversary of *Best Canadian Essays* and my third as series editor. I've been lucky to inherit the work of my predecessor Alex Boyd and to work with excellent guest editors Ibi Kaslik, Ray Robertson and now essayist and novelist Stephen Marche in selecting the works for inclusion. Naturally, I have them to thank along with Halli Villegas, Carolina Smart, Nathaniel Moore and everyone else at Tightrope Books for the opportunity to read works from across the country and check the barometer of peoples' concerns.

With the recent popularity of the essay form, there has been some hand wringing about its direction as a whole, particularly in the United States. From Christy Wampole's "The Essayification of Everything" in the *New York Times* (discussed at length in this volume's introduction) to Adam Kirsch's assertion in the *New Republic* that "the new essay is exclusively about the self, with the world serving only as a foil and an accessory, as a mere staging ground for the projection of the self," positioning the essay as yet another narcissistic outlet for an increasingly self-absorbed society. Kirsch laments that the 'new essayist,'—he counts Sloane Crosley, John Jeremiah Sullivan, Davy Rothbart and their forebear, the immensely popular David Sedaris among their number—is a sort of quirky bumbler who flaunts his comic ineptitude, often to the point of straining credulity, in a variety of situations for the amusement, as opposed to enlightenment, of a superficial reading public.

That Canada does not produce, or perhaps reward, this type of essayist can be seen in a number of lights. One could view it as Canadian writers perversely ignoring that specific portion of the popular marketplace where the essay thrives. One could see it as a symptom of the serious tone generally adopted by Canadian magazines and journals; say what one will about Canadians but we are rarely thought of as playful. If one views it through the lens of audience expectation, Canadian readers are either more introspective and 'deeper' than their American counterparts or hopelessly out of touch as to where the essay currently sits. One could see it as an example of American individualism versus Canadian collectivism: one writer wants to document what happened to him, the other what happened to us. Consequently, it could also be that the US writer, aided by the press, has often benefitted from the idea of the singular, forceful personality where the Canadian writer is expected to be publically self-effacing (when this has not been the case—see Irving Layton and Mordecai Richler—Canadians get uncomfortable and are asked by the writer's supporters and apologists to forget about the personality and focus on the work) out of a mixture of genuine humility and fear of tall poppy syndrome, an ugly place for a writer to live. One could even see it as petulant Canadian cultural reactionism: what they like we don't and that defines our tastes.

I imagine the answer amounts to a combination of all these and more but also a difference in our notions of performative writing. If the current crop of US essayists is intent on injecting themselves into their subject matter, indeed until they become the subject matter, the Canadian essayist performs the work simply by writing it. The new US essayist intends to destabilize what is 'real' both by exposure of the writer as unreliable persona and by exposing the mechanics of essay-writing itself (as James Wood put it in *The New Yorker*, "the contemporary essay likes to display its postmodernity by showing us its workings"), the Canadian essayist still believes in the ability to express himself without guile, but still with an awareness of that very lack of guile, which either indicates a healthy contrarian spirit or a stunning lack of sophistication on the part of Canadian writers depending on your point of view. I doubt that it is an accident that after he derided the work of the new essayists, Kirsch went on to praise Toronto's Sheila Heti for blending autobiography and fiction to illuminate a genuine self. The essays presented here all convey something to the reader without the interlocutions of self-reflexive chicanery and perhaps that is their strength. This year our writers chose to express themselves by going directly at their subjects whether it be the generation gap (Sanati and Kaeser), Canada's relationship with the rest of the world (Turner and Welsh), how best to memorialize the dead (Connelly, Dizdar and Gemma), the state of literary culture and other works of art (Robertson and Friesen), or any of the other topics covered. As the debate over the essay's direction continues, next year, who knows?

Christopher Doda

Introduction

The essay is the form of our moment. Increasingly, the essayist—more even than the novelist or the scriptwriter—is the aspirational model of the writer. In Lena Dunham's *Girls*, which is itself much more successful as a source for essays than as an actual television show, the lead character Hannah dreams, not of making movies or writing the Great American Novel, but of publishing longform personal recollections and cultural analysis. Essays are a way in for kid writers and a way for mature writers to make a living—whether through popular pieces in magazines or scholarly articles for academia. Everyone learns how to write by writing essays in school; essayists are the ones who just don't stop.

Christy Wampole, in "The Essayification of Everything," an essay about essays on the subject of essays for *The New York Times*, recently investigated what cultural motivations lurked behind the triumph of the genre:

> It seems that, even in the proliferation of new forms of writing and communication before us, the essay has become a talisman of our times. What is behind our attraction to it? Is it the essay's therapeutic properties? Because it brings miniature joys to its writer and its reader? Because it is small enough to fit in our pocket, portable like our own experiences?

The technological revolution which has so disrupted other media has been a major beneficiary to the essay. Never have we had the means to read so much great material, so instantly. A recent symposium, organized by *PORT magazine*, which included the editors of *The New York Times Magazine* and *Vanity Fair* heralded 'a golden age of magazines,' largely because print products have been joined by online and tablet editions. There are just so many new ways to put work in the public eye today and for the reading public to find great work. It's extraordinary how much technology is devoted either to creating small essays or to consuming them. And not just through websites like Longreads. We live in the time of the link, it's true, but what people link to is essays. Twitter is essentially a never-ending, continuous anthology.

In its original sense, derived from Montaigne four hundred years ago, an "essay" means an attempt, a term both complimentary and derogatory. A good essay is nothing more than an attempt but it's also a genuine effort into understanding the way things work. In a world of constantly shifting, changeable and urgent information, a world of grandiose claims and rampant narcissism, we need the humble essay more than ever. Built into the form itself is a kind of humility and a hope of freshness, a journey into the unexpected and the unknown, and also an act of daring. That optimistic but skeptical spirit is, I believe, the key to the current triumph of the form. The virtues of the essay have never been more necessary than they are at this moment in history. They are also the virtues found in *Best Canadian Essays* this year.

Canadian literature is certainly more famous for its collection of novelists and short story writers than it is for its essayists, which makes sense: a country starved of national myths needs fabulists and conjurers more than debunkers and critics. Or at least it did. The country's emerging postnationalist literary maturity as much as its multicultural reality demands the essay more and more for its capacity to hold a variety of perspectives.

The geographical variety of the country is reflected in pieces as far apart as Katherine Laidlaw's investigative piece on The Giant Mine Strike in Yellowknife, "Murder in the Mine," for *Up Here Magazine* and Chris Turner's essay on the more than a million Canadians who annually enjoy the morally dubious advantages of the super-cheap beach holiday, "On Tipping in Cuba" for *The Walrus*. 4,988 kilometres separate the settings of those stories— Yellowknife and Havana—but they are both about the hidden costs of Canadian economic decisions.

Intellectual variety, no less than geographical variety, is also on display. There are reports from the front line of a changing culture, such as Michelle Kaeser's report on the generational war, "Hello I'm Screwed" for *This Magazine*, Denise Balkisoon's "The Bully Mob" for *Toronto Life*, and Maryam Sanati's "Brand Me," (incidentally also a fascinating report of the changing nature of the essay itself). There are studies of forgotten works of art, like Eric Friesen's "A Tangle of Rainbows: A *Quartet* for the End of Time," on the composer Olivier Messiaen. There are philosophical approaches to pressing questions such as Mark Kingwell's "Building Cities, Making Friends" from that always reliably brilliant repository of the Canadian essay *Queen's Quarterly*. There are analyses of foreign policy, such as Jennifer Welsh's "Beyond War and Peacekeeping" for *The Literary Review of Canada*.

The variety of material and the variety of approaches to the material is extraordinary, from straight-up reporting to philosophy, memoir and polemic. In addition, *Best Canadian Essays 2013* has some fascinating examples of my favourite type of essay, the uncategorizable kind that fuses the personal, the political, the sociological and the lyrical with whatever else the writer can throw into the mixture. The results are sometimes staggering. Karen Connelly's "Washing the Body" for *Alberta Views* is an unforgettable description of the death of her mother. "Harrowing" is an overused word, but Sierra Sky Gemma's "The Wrong Way" from *The New Quarterly* cannot really be described any other way. Similarly strange and powerful are Robert Finley's "The Approaches" and Wayne Grady's "On the Willing Suspension of Disbelief," the latter of which almost feels like it had to be an essay because it couldn't be anything else.

Essays, among all genres, are unique in their openness to material. Short story material is like uranium. You have to search forever to find it, and when you do you have to extract it, excruciatingly, and then refine it endlessly. Writing a novel is like passing a season in the mines. But the essay is made with what you find on the ground. From material as diverse as Bosnian gravesites, or a view of the sea or a Cuban mojito, arguments about the whole world suddenly emerge.

It is traditional, at this point in the discussion of any Canadian cultural phenomenon, to start complaining. Writers in our country are supposed to be survivors, just hanging on. So I should, I guess, talk about threats to creative industries and basically bitch and moan about how hard it is to be a writer. But I think on the whole, such pessimism would be out of place in a preface to a collection such as this anyway, which is so full of reasons for hope. The most exciting feature of *Best Canadian Essays 2013* is that it looks like we're just at the beginning, the beginning of something great.

In "The Essayification of Everything," Wampole worries that the rise of the essay may be evidence of a new narcissism, of an obsession with the self. I think that conjecture may be an exaggeration but it also puts a finger on the pulse of the essay's strength. The essays in this book are the world filtered through the self. The personal nature of the essay and its lack of constraints will inevitably produce eccentricity, which is a major asset. Wampole comes to this conclusion herself:

> [The essay's] spirit resists closed-ended, hierarchical thinking and encourages both writer and reader to postpone their verdict on life. It is an invitation to maintain the elasticity of mind and to get comfortable with the world's inherent ambivalence. And, most importantly, it is an imaginative rehearsal of what isn't but could be.

The essay may be the form of the moment, but it is, more than that, a signal to the future. It is in that spirit that the selections for *Best Canadian Essays 2013* should be taken. They emanate a certain kind of hope, a hope that by trying we can understand and possibly even change.

Stephen Marche

Best Canadian Essays
2013

The Bully Mob

Denise Balkissoon

Mitchell Wilson had a short life. He was born in March 2000 at Markham-Stouffville Hospital to Craig and Shelley Wilson. From the age of three, he had trouble running and jumping. He climbed stairs slowly, putting both feet on each step before moving up. He fell often, and sometimes he couldn't get up on his own. His doctors thought he had hypermobility syndrome—joints that extend and bend more than normal.

When Mitchell was seven, his mother was diagnosed with an aggressive melanoma. Her treatments left her distant, sometimes testy and mean, and in so much pain that she rarely left her bedroom. "I sort of kept Mitchell away," Craig Wilson told me. "He basically didn't talk to his mother during the last four months of her life." Wilson often left his son to his own devices while he took care of his dying wife and ran his family's industrial knife business. Mitchell spent most of his time in his bedroom, playing video games. He comforted himself with food, and by the time he was four feet tall he weighed 167 pounds. Once, in a Walmart, he fell to the ground and his grandmother had to ask store employees to help her lift him.

In 2010, Craig Wilson remarried, to a woman named Tiffany Usher. After a campy Las Vegas ceremony during which they both wore flip-flops, the couple moved with Mitchell and Usher's two preteen daughters into a four-bedroom house just east of Rouge Park. Usher had worked as a special education teacher, and she suspected that Mitchell's hypermobility syndrome diagnosis wasn't right. She took him to SickKids, where doctors determined he had a type of muscular dystrophy called limb girdle, a genetic disease that eats away at the muscle tissue in the shoulders and hips. Mitchell's parents didn't tell him that he'd probably die in his mid-twenties, and that he'd spend his last couple of years in bed, breathing with the help of a respirator.

Muscular dystrophy usually brings with it cognitive limitations. Mitchell was labelled gifted in math but severely learning disabled in languages. This, along with his weight and his bright red hair, made him a target for teasing at Pickering's William Dunbar P.S. Mitchell was ridiculed when he fell, and he was sometimes knocked down to be laughed at as he struggled to his feet. Other students would step on him, then give each other high-fives.

The Wilsons transferred Mitchell to Westcreek P.S. for Grade 5, and he seemed happier. He became known as a goof, even a troublemaker—he was regularly kicked out of French class for encouraging other students to tease the teacher by making silly sounds and faces. He found a group of friends, including a skateboarder named Max, who was in Grade 8. Having an older friend gave him confidence. Once, Max taught Mitchell how to jam the school elevator so that he'd have an excuse to skip his second-floor classes.

The only therapy to slow Mitchell's muscle loss was exercise. He swam at the Pickering rec centre and spent hours walking around his subdivision. When he sat he wore leg braces to help his muscles stretch. In the fall of 2010, he borrowed his dad's iPhone to listen to music on one of his walks. His stepmom was driving through a nearby housing complex when she spotted Mitchell. She also saw two older, bigger kids approach him. One of the boys, now known to the court system as J. S., pushed him to the ground and snatched the iPhone. Mitchell chipped two of his front teeth and was bleeding from scraped knees but was otherwise okay. Usher called the police, then took Mitchell to the hospital. J. S. was arrested two days later.

The incident made Mitchell anxious and self-conscious. He cut down on his walks and swims. His dad took him to sessions with counsellors to help him cope with his health problems, his mom's death and his attack, but he stubbornly refused to talk. He also refused when his parents suggested he sign up for a summer camp where he could mingle with other kids who have mobility restrictions.

Last summer, Mitchell told his parents he wasn't looking forward to Grade 6. His friend Max had graduated, and he knew he'd be lonely. "I'll kill myself if I have to go back to school," he said during a trip to the family cottage. "He said that every year," said Wilson. "He said it last year, and the year before that. We never thought for a minute that he would act on it." A subpoena for Mitchell to testify against J. S. in court arrived on Labour Day. Mitchell would have to face his attacker and relive the experience in a room full of strangers. His dad sent him to bed that night with encouraging words about a new year of school and a fresh start.

Sometime in the middle of the night, Mitchell tied a plastic bag over his head. When Craig went to wake his son up for school the next morning, he found Mitchell's lifeless body and screamed so loud the rest of the family came running. Usher called 911.

What stunned Mitchell's parents most about his suicide was how determined he must have been. "There was no hesitation, no 'I want another hug,'" Wilson said of his son's last night. "There were no extra 'I love yous.'" Mitchell didn't leave a note.

A peculiar thing happened to Mitchell Wilson in the weeks that followed his death: he became famous. Not famous as a kid who suffered from muscular dystrophy. Not famous as a kid who was mugged for an iPhone. He became known as the 11-year-old who was so afraid of the bullies at school that he took his own life.

On September 22, Mitchell's photo appeared on the front page of the *Sun* under the headline "Bullied to Death." Similar stories followed in the *Star*, in the *Post* and on TV news. Mitchell's parents were frustrated by what they saw as an oversimplification of his death. "What happened to Mitchell—being assaulted and robbed—that's not bullying, that's a criminal act," says Usher. The attack had taken place off school property, yet the news stories portrayed the case as an example of out-of-control schoolyard bullying. Wilson has a theory on why the media latched on to the bullying aspect of his son's story: "When an 11-year-old takes their own life, it leaves you with a lot of questions," he says. "People want a simple label and a simple answer. Putting the word 'suicide' out in the open creates a lot of fear."

Wilson might be right, but there are other factors at play, too. Parents, teachers and bureaucrats see bullying everywhere. What was once a term to describe a playground fight now applies to all manner of harassment, from homophobic and racist taunts to nasty Facebook comments. Today, kids are taught that it's their responsibility to immediately report the faintest hint of bullying behaviour. Researchers at Queen's University who track the health of Canadian children for the World Health Organization found, in a 2006 study, that twenty-one percent of boys and twenty-four percent of girls in Grade 8 said they had been bullied at least once in the past week.

A series of highly publicized deaths turned bullying into the hot-button issue it is today. In 1997, Reena Virk, the 14-year-old daughter of Indian immigrants, was beaten by eight teens in Saanich, B.C., then forcibly drowned. The next year, Myles Neuts, a 10-year-old from Chatham, Ontario, suffocated and died after he was hung by other students on a coat hook in the washroom of his school. In 2000, Dawn-Marie Wesley, a 14-year-old from Mission, B.C., committed suicide and left a note blaming three female students who regularly bullied her. Since then, a number of suicides across the country have been attributed to bullying, including those of Joshua Melo, a 15-year-old from Strathroy, Ontario, in 2004, Brendan Deleary, a 15-year-old from London, Ontario, in 2010, and Jenna Bowers-Bryanton, a 15-year-old from Belmont, Nova Scotia, in 2011.

Just two weeks after Mitchell Wilson killed himself, a 15-year-old Ottawa student named Jamie Hubley, who had endured years of cruel homophobic taunts at school and online, committed suicide. The CBC comedian Rick Mercer, commenting on Hubley's death, implored prominent Canadians to lead by example by coming out of the closet.

The concern with bullying has spawned an entire industry of school programs, television specials, radio documentaries and pundits eager to discuss how to protect kids. In 1997, a former vice-principal named Stu Auty brought together a group of educators, police officers and parents to form the Canadian Safe School Network, which bills itself as an arm's-length research and advocacy group for reducing school violence. Since 2003, schools across the country have taken part in an annual bullying awareness week in November, and a one-off anti-bullying day that started in Nova

Scotia (students wore pink T-shirts to protest homophobic intimidation) has grown into a tradition across the country.

Whether or not schools perceive a problem, they have no choice but to embrace anti-bullying measures to guard against legal liability. In 1996, a B.C. teenager named Azmi Jubran filed a complaint with the B.C. Human Rights Commission, alleging that teachers and principals at Handsworth Secondary hadn't done enough to protect him from five years of homophobic bullying. Although the tribunal awarded him only $4,500, the North Vancouver school board appealed the decision on the grounds that Jubran wasn't, in fact, gay. The case reached B.C.'s Court of Appeal in 2005, which upheld the original tribunal decision. The court also found that the bullies had violated the dignity and equality statutes of the Human Rights Code, and that the school board had failed to provide Jubran with a learning environment free from discriminatory harassment.

Jubran's lawsuit was precedent-setting. Schools prepared for a flood of suits, and they came. In 2002, a Burlington teen named David Knight filed a $500,000 suit after classmates set up a website to taunt him and his family. Knight claimed that educators at his school knew about the site (which described him as a pedophile, among other things) and failed to act. Aside from the money, he wanted a public apology and a commitment from the board to taking a tougher stance on bullying in the future. The case settled out of court for an undisclosed sum.

A Toronto-based personal injury lawyer named Daniela Cervini is currently handling eight bullying lawsuits against Ontario school boards, including two against the TDSB. Her firm, Grillo Barristers, receives calls on a weekly basis from parents wanting to take legal action against bullies and the school officials who didn't do enough to stop them. Cervini is asking for an average of $8.5 million in damages for each case. "The children need counselling to get back on track," she says, "and that's expensive." She's representing kids ranging from kindergarten age to high school level in claims that run the gamut from teasing to sexual assault. One student in the Halton Catholic School Board was beaten by a group of classmates, a video of the assault posted on YouTube. When Cervini's cases make it to court, she'll argue bullying incidents that happen off school property are still the school's responsibility, because bullies whose behaviour is ignored in class become emboldened after the bell rings. In her experience, many teachers and principals aren't following the anti-bullying rules that school boards are so eager to tout. In one instance, a student was beaten with sticks in the school playground and the principal didn't notify the police.

Cervini believes that perhaps "bullying" is too mild a word for what some of these kids have gone through, but she says the term has gained enough traction in recent years to make it useful. "Bullying finally has widespread attention," she says. "People are standing up to the schools."

Both Durham District schools Mitchell Wilson attended have an elaborate anti-bullying policy. Like other Ontario boards, Durham has developed a detailed safety policy to address bullying, which is defined by the Ministry of Education as "a form of repeated, persistent and aggressive behaviour directed at an individual or individuals that is intended to cause (or should be known to cause) fear and distress and/or harm to another person's body, feelings, self-esteem or reputation." Ontario schools practise a so-called progressive discipline process that emphasizes rehabilitation. It was legislated into existence by the province in 2008 to replace the Harris government's punitive "zero tolerance" policy—which was criticized for encouraging a rash of expulsions.

Between 2004 and 2012, the Ministry of Education distributed $30 million to Ontario school boards to combat bullying. The province maintains a registry for teachers and principals of 129 recommended anti-bullying workshops, professional speakers and programs. The options are wide-ranging: there's a $15 anti-Islamophobia kit from a Muslim outreach group called Mentors; a two-day, $2,400 Red Cross workshop called "Beyond the Hurt"; and sessions on gangs, life with a military parent and homophobia. The non-profit Ontario Physical and Health Education Association is paid ($15,000 in the last year) to assess whether the programs suit current curriculum objectives, but the sessions are not formally evaluated by the government.

More than ever, schools are taking responsibility for nurturing the emotional health of their students. The newest anti-bullying programs focus on "character development," or what Lisa Millar, Pickering's superintendent of education, describes as "producing good citizens." In Durham, students from kindergarten through Grade 12 are now taught ten character traits they're meant to cultivate throughout their public school years: teamwork, responsibility, respect, perseverance, optimism, kindness, integrity, honesty, empathy and courage. The TDSB promises students "ongoing support and professional growth in emotional intelligence." Private schools such as Branksome Hall and Upper Canada College have similar goals. Branksome instituted a new anti-bullying policy that reminds students that what happens online—Facebook was found to be overrun with bullying behaviour—has consequences in the real world.

One of the most popular programs on the province's registry is called Roots of Empathy. A former educator named Mary Gordon founded the program and has held sessions for 200,000 Toronto children since 1996. The province spent $2 million from 2009 to 2011 to bring Roots of Empathy to Ontario students. The program has earned many accolades: Gordon has met with the Dalai Lama three times, and she has won, among other awards, the Queen's Golden Jubilee Medal for commitment to education. Her program has spread throughout the U.K. and Ireland, as well as to New Zealand and the U.S. She was skeptical of anti-bullying approaches that focused exclusively on punishing the perpetrator. "Humiliating children never works," she tells me. "Pretty much every approach before now hasn't been effective."

At the core of Roots of Empathy is a baby. Gordon recruits moms to bring their new offspring into classrooms in order to teach students about vulnerability and feelings. She believes that observing and interacting with the baby will teach children how to identify and articulate their feelings and those of others around them. They will learn that other people can also feel sad, or lonely—which Gordon says is often a revelation for them—and that while it's okay to be angry or frustrated, there are acceptable and unacceptable ways to deal with unpleasant feelings.

The TDSB doesn't collect data on whether Roots has reduced fights or suspensions, but Gordon is attempting to do so herself. Her program has commissioned surveys of students and teachers about classroom behaviour before and after the sessions—one 2001 finding from Manitoba showed that twenty-seven sessions resulted in a thirty-nine percent decrease in aggression and a sixty-five percent increase in sharing. Gordon also believes she can prove her program changes the very structure and functioning of a child's brain, effectively altering emotional development. This school year, with the help of York University, she's conducting a new round of research with a foray into neuroscience. Researchers will use a non-invasive technique to study the emotional response centres of students' brains before and after the Roots of Empathy program.

There is some proof anti-bullying campaigns that focus on character development and strategic discipline have an impact. After a series of youth suicides in Norway in the early 1980s, a University of Bergen psychology professor named Dan Olweus surveyed thousands of students about bullying, then developed his eponymous anti-bullying program. He now works in the U.S., where the Olweus program is rabidly popular. Part of the approach involves setting out clear rules about bullying, making sure they are communicated often to students and staff, and sticking to a discipline plan. The rest involves "reducing antisocial behaviour" and "improving the school climate"; in other words, pursuing the ambitious and abstract goal of fertilizing emotional intelligence at a tender age in order to eradicate bullying in the future. The Olweus program boasts staggering numbers—in a study of 2,500 students over two and a half years, it was shown to reduce bullying by fifty percent at forty-two different schools.

The influential Harvard psychology professor Steven Pinker has proposed that the need for anti-bullying programs is exaggerated—because there's less bullying happening today than ever before. Last fall, Pinker published *The Better Angels of Our Nature*, a provocative and controversial book that combines psychological studies with his readings of history and neuroscience to make a solid argument that we live in the least violent era in all of human history. There are fewer wars and fewer deaths in the wars that do happen, and by all accounts, rates of everything from homicide to domestic violence to, yes, bullying are drastically lower than ever before, especially in the developed world. Pinker cites school statistics from the U.S. departments of justice and education, which revealed that less than ten percent of youths reported crimes or feeling fear at school in 2003. A 2007 statistical survey by the same departments showed that the rate had dropped even further, to five percent .

Pinker uses his findings to criticize what he calls the "empathy craze." He points to the dozens of self-help bestsellers of recent years that focus on the subject, including Gordon's own *Roots of Empathy: Changing the World Child by Child*, which he mocks for its jacket promise to strive for "no less than world peace." Pinker believes we need more than empathy to snuff out violence. He cites various experiments and studies he claims show that person-to-person empathy will always, no matter what, be at least partially dependent on considerations like good looks, similarity and communal solidarity. Instinctive knowledge of this might be why it's hard for bystanders to stand up to bullying, since adolescence is a time when we especially crave fitting in. Empathy has a role to play in violence reduction, Pinker says, but more important in his mind has been the rise in recognition of basic human rights, and societies' commitment to defending those rights. In Pinker's opinion, the drop in school bullying in the U.S. is due far more to the recognition of children's right to live without violence, and the willingness of schools to enforce it. In other words, the most effective way to stop bullying is with old-fashioned law and order.

To the parents of a bullied kid, schools can't do enough to prevent or punish bullying. What they don't want to hear is that bullying is ignored or tolerated. And what they never want to see is another bullying death.

About a month after Mitchell Wilson's suicide, Craig Wilson and Tiffany Usher received a call from a booker for *Dr. Phil*. The show wanted them to come to L.A. to tell Mitchell's story, which would make Dr. Phil's audience coo and gasp in heartbreak and outrage. A day or so later, Dr. Phil's people sent an email. The lineup for the bullying show had grown, and there wasn't time to interview the couple live. Instead, the show would send over a video camera and a list of printed questions. Wilson was instructed to give heartfelt answers about Mitchell's suicide to the camera. It was obvious they wanted to milk his tragedy. "They wanted me to cry," Wilson says, "so I told them to go fuck themselves."

After Mitchell's death, Westcreek P.S. was scrutinized as a hotbed of prejudice and neglect. Pickering parents seemed to believe that, despite all the anti-bullying campaigns and empathy instruction, the school hadn't done enough to create a safe environment for a vulnerable kid, and they demanded that Westcreek's principal, Tony Rizzuto, be held accountable. Why, people asked, aren't Mitchell's parents suing the school? Usher and Wilson were surprised by the backlash: they had no plans to sue Rizzuto or the school. They say that Mitchell was deeply fond of Rizzuto, who looked out for him. The day after Mitchell was assaulted, J. S. was taken out of the public school system. And a week later, when one of J. S.'s friends, in a vengeful mood, taunted Mitchell, Wilson and Usher reported to Rizzuto what happened and he immediately called the harassing student's parents. Rizzuto had also given Mitchell's friend Max permission to hang out with him indoors during recess (Mitchell avoided the playground). He delivered a eulogy at Mitchell's funeral at the Pickering Village United Church.

A few weeks later, Wilson stood in front of the Durham school board to register his support of Rizzuto and ask that trustees ignore the unfounded complaints. The board decided Rizzuto didn't require discipline.

Yes, Mitchell was bullied, and it hurt, but his school didn't neglect him. Mitchell was surrounded by empathy: he had friends and a family who loved him. What he didn't have was peace with the fact that he'd never be an average kid. Wilson and Usher suspect their son Googled his disease. He'd have discovered that his rapidly approaching end would be miserable. After the loss of his mother, after years of humiliation for his disability, his prognosis might have been one too many heartbreaks for an 11-year-old to take.

Washing the Body

Karen Connelly

While she was dying, there was often silence-without-silence. We wanted it to end. Yet we could not bear the thought of it ending. Agonized breathing repeated its small history. Smoking. Years working in a lead-contaminated police headquarters; the lead from the bullets in the basement firing range filtered up, circulated, entered the nose, the throat, the lungs of everyone who worked there. She used to come home with the bad news of a workmate's miscarriage, a stillbirth, another baby born with cerebral palsy.

The flesh inside her throat was ruined. The radiation stripped off what the cancer didn't destroy. It was like slag coming away inside her. She coughed and choked it up, but the mucus came back quickly, stretched its sticky web through her throat. None of us could escape the belaboured, ragged sound of her breathing.

Sometimes we sat and looked at each other, but sometimes we talked. Or she would be asleep and we, any number of her four children and one grandchild-almost daughter, would discuss, or whine, or argue. Twice she surprised us by chiming in, "Oh, the garden, it's so beautiful, isn't it?" Though she could not see it. She expressed often and easily her love for us. "Hers is a happy textbook case," said the head nurse, and I wasn't sure whether to be gratified or insulted. My mother? A textbook case?

But it was true. She had set her house in order. Literally. She had returned to her exacting god and her three younger sisters, from whom she'd been estranged for years. She had forgiven and been forgiven. I admired that she'd waited until the last possible moment to rejoin the religious fold; it was kind of her to spare us her children the headache of Jehovah and the difficult aunts. But, dying, she loved them again, she made peace, and prayed, and smiled often, even through grimaces. Once she entered Rosedale Hospice and had better pain medication than at home, she fairly glowed. Not because she was on a drug high—she was allergic to morphine—but because she was so happy to be poised at the edge of death.

She was not sentimental or upset about leaving her little home in northeast Calgary; her belongings were already labelled with names, parcelled out to her children and friends. Rosedale Hospice is a big, beautiful house, formerly a seminary, its high-ceilinged chapel still intact. She loved being there because it stands on a high northwestern rim of the Bow River valley. If she could have stood on the chair behind the garage—as I often did—she would have had a view down the steep bluffs to the river of her childhood, the neighbourhood of Sunnyside where she was raised, the four stone lions guarding the Centre Street Bridge. When she was a child, her uncle used to walk with her over that bridge, tap his cane against one of the great plinths, then give her the sweets that the lions had magically placed in his pockets.

She couldn't see any of it anymore. She could barely get out of bed. She would never see any of it again. But she knew exactly where the hospice was. We had told her that the big house was surrounded by trees, by gardens. She had been a great gardener; it was a fitting place for her to die.

And for us to sit and wait. There is a guestroom for out-of-town visitors, so I was able to stay there for several days—a week? More?—and walk the bluffs, and meander down into Kensington for a look at the foreign, busy world of the living, espresso machines and cars, gorgeous young summery men and women, bookshops. Though I saw people I had gone to school with, no one recognized me. I did not recognize myself.

I had never felt so regretful. I was the responsible but geographically distant daughter. I had been away from the country for many years, and now lived, of all traitorous eastern lands, in *Toronto*. Why didn't I take her to Greece? I tried. The tickets were booked, the hotels. It was the summer she got sick. I had waited too long. Why didn't I bring her with me again to Thailand? She laughed. "Don't be ridiculous. I never felt like you abandoned me. You've all been such good children. I've had such a treasure in my children."

I smiled indulgently, turning my head away to roll my eyes. What about the drug addict? And the quasi-professional thief? What about the years of prison visits and stolen money?

She seemed to read my mind, and sighed, "You've all turned out so well." She could afford to let everything go, after all; she was on her way out. But she had always been like that. A classic enabler, when it came to addicts, but also honestly, deeply generous, to almost everyone. *Some people have nothing*, she used to say. *Look how rich I am.* She had five children, three grandchildren. A small two-bedroom townhouse, an old car. Her garden. A few friends. She meant her happiness. And, practically, three meals a day, a winter coat, a safe home. Her riches were the riches many people have, but which do not suffice, do not staunch greed and restlessness. Though a lapsed Christian for decades, she was actually an animist Buddhist by nature. It was hard to live up to her essential goodness, though the gratitude seemed like a genetic trait she had passed on to us. We have each of us felt blessed to have been born, and, especially, to have been born her children. There was a significant measure of misery in our childhoods, but while she was dying we remembered almost exclusively her joy, the joy and kindness we learned from her. She smiled at me, her eyes shining, her polished-looking knuckles under my fingers, cool and round as marbles. I stroked them compulsively. "Now, especially, I only see what is good in each of you. I love you all so much."

Frankly, I wanted to be loved the most. The child I had been strained against my adult skin, wanting to crawl into bed with her mother. But there was no room, and the tubes got in the way. I pulled my chair closer and searched her thin, unfamiliar, familiar, beautiful face, thrilled because my other siblings weren't there. Of all the minutes yet to come in my life, I could have my mother to myself for thirty-five more of them.

Soon after that, she dropped into unconsciousness. Her struggle for breath worsened and sent us each, in turn, fleeing from her room, agitated or angry or in tears. "Can't you do something?" we asked—we begged—the nurses. "She's suffering!" Yet looking back at that time, just a year and a half ago, I don't know if she was suffering all that much. But we certainly were. The worst fights erupted then, the most awful accusations were levelled. Who had loved her more, who had neglected her when she was sick. We carved it up, the five of us, and gave each other a portion of our loss.

The late summer garden of Rosedale Hospice grew and grew. In between the bouts of intensity and taking distracted, hasty care of some of the business of life, we sat out in the back garden, behind the garage, where old wicker chairs stood in various stages of collapse on the small patio. The attendants told us to go ahead, eat the raspberries, eat the tomatoes, and we did. We had halting conversations with other dying people, and hilariously black-humoured chats with the attendants, who came to sit out back on their breaks. There was a week of that, our mother inside unconscious, not eating, not drinking, all the tubes except the pain relief pulled out. She was trying hard to die, but her heart was strong and her body stronger. As at the unknowable beginnings of our lives, we were once again suspended inside her strength, waiting. We waited through afternoons that seemed endless and evenings that opened, deepened, became bluer and bluer until that shocking made-in-Alberta blue bloomed above the city and night breathed out the scent of dry grass and dust. It came from the hillside, that smell. When I stood on one of the chairs (fearing at every moment that my foot would break through the ruined wicker) I could see the river below, glinting darkly under the lights of downtown. It was so beautiful, the city, the sky, the night, and our mother was almost gone.

We were sitting out there one afternoon when a nurse called us in: "She's going." I thought of a boat moving away, how it gets smaller and smaller, disappears. The person left standing on the dock has nowhere to go. Does any other horizon mean more than that one? We came into the house to kiss her and hug her and hold her hands as she went. Throughout my life, sitting at her kitchen table, she had taught me how to travel well.

I thought her body would become silent and cold almost immediately. I thought some part of me would become cold and silent also. But it takes hours for the heat to leave a newly dead person. My siblings were amazed when I told the hospice attendant that I wanted to help wash and dress my mother for the funeral home. I said to my sister, "You *don't* want to help?" Possibly inspired by the criminal element in our family, she has become a cop, so she regularly sees the corpses of those who did not want to die. I thought she'd like to spend more time with our mother, who had been anxious to depart, and well-prepared. But I was wrong. "Are you nuts? I'm going out for a smoke."

The hospice attendant was also surprised, but tremulously pleased, despite her anxious expression. (Did she think I would howl and tear my hair?) I undressed my mother. Her body looked pretty good. "I'm so healthy except for this damn cancer," she often said, rightly. She wasn't very old-looking for 69, though the recent surgery and the work of dying had exhausted her. As I gazed fondly at her pale stretch marks, the small, loose breasts that had nursed us, I thought again how much the work of dying resembles the labour of birth. I had given birth to my son less than two years before and the experiences shimmered side by side in my consciousness, two fresh-caught fish on a sunlit table.

The waiting, the sleeplessness, the altered sense of self. The bloody hard work of it all, the extraordinary *task*, so grand and so mundane. The way it brings everything up, like existential peristalsis, unstoppable: the buried family darkness, the longings and fears, the physical weaknesses and hidden strengths. All is vomited onto the hard surface of those extreme moments. Even if we succeed in hiding it, it is still there. And at the end, there is a prize, a gift. Everyone who comes to this place receive it. Twice. For those attending to the labourer as well as for the one crossing the threshold, the sharp awareness of breath is central. Simple breath is the force that accomplishes all, and, in ceasing, ends all.

How oddly comforting I found these similarities, partly because they proved how true poetry is *(I knew it!)*: metaphors are everywhere, in everything. Metaphor is *encoded* in us. There is an almost scientific indivisibility in human experience. Loops and loops of connection hold us together as individuals, as a race, even as a species in the ecosystem. Life itself becomes the placenta that feeds us as we begin to die. I wished that the hospice had a poetry section in addition to their thriller, mystery and new-age library, because I wanted to re-read the whole of T. S. Eliot's "The Gift of the Magi." But the few lines I knew by heart served me well:

> I had seen birth
> and death
> and thought they were different.
> Were we led all that way
> for birth or death?

All that way. How hard my mother's life had been. How far she had walked. Yet she had the most beautiful legs and feet, like a 30-year-old's, more shapely than my own. Not a single varicose vein. I laughed as I washed her legs, her feet, wringing the cloth in the plastic basin of warm water, drying her with a towel. "Look how great this nail polish looks," I said to the attendant, gesturing at my mother's toenails, which were painted gold. "She's still so warm," I said again. We had to use lotion to loosen the rings on her fingers. They still wouldn't come off. We pulled and twisted; her hands had swelled. We used soap. I had the big amber antique-looking one and the attendant worked on the yellow gold one. It seemed impossible to me that all that rubbing and yanking didn't hurt her. But she didn't cry out. In death as in life, she remained stoic.

But not silent. She was dead, finally. She had told me that what I needed of her I already had. She said that when she was dead, I would begin to feel the shape of her, a sort of template, a presence I would carry around. "The same thing happened when my own mother died," she told me. I had nodded a lot, thinking she was getting nostalgic. But I suddenly understood what she meant. The rings slid off her fingers unexpectedly, one after the other, as if she had decided to let them go. The gold one was for my niece; the amber one was for my sister-in-law, whom I don't like. So I wished it had remained on her finger. But I slipped them both into my pocket, prepared to fulfill my daughterly duty.

The attendant and I changed the water in our plastic basins. I made sure it was warm. I carefully washed her face. It was the last time I would see her face complete, fully her own, because a medical specialist was coming soon to remove her eyes. Typical. Waste not, want not. She'd told us, "Well, I don't need them anymore, do I?"

I stroked her cheek with my fingers. The attendant turned away for a moment. Then she put her hand on my arm, and looked into my eyes. She was in her early 50s, with shoulder-length dark hair, an attractive, almost girlish face. "I want you to know that this is the best way you could honour your mother."

Honour. Such a neglected, old word. I smiled and said, "I love her. I love this body." I put one hand on my mother's shoulder, the other hand on her head of short, dry hair. As if the attendant might doubt my provenance, I declared, "I came from this body!" The adult now, I wanted to gather her whole into my arms, embrace all that she had ever been. Keep her. The gift, the gift! She had made me from her blood, from the darkness at the crux of her; she had spun my flesh and bone.

Once, when I was a child, she told me about a walk she took along the Bow River. She thought she was about eight years old then, which was the age I was when she told me how something had happened to her that day. An event took place that sustained her for the rest of her life. Even as a small child, she often walked by the river; her family lived just across Memorial Drive. But on that day, something stopped her on the riverbank. She smelled wolf willow and felt the cold water hurtling by. The moment caught and held her still. She felt in her skin and her bones that she belonged to the sharp morning air and the shining trees. Like the fish she couldn't see, she was part of the river. "To know this," she said, "meant that everything would be all right. It was as though God was standing beside me. God was standing everywhere."

Jackie Lebbert Henry was her name. "Everything will be all right" was the practical motto of her life. For months, her ashes rested in a box in my sister's closet, beneath her uniform shirts. We sent some of them to my brother. I kept a box myself. Then, last October, I returned to Calgary in the midst of a big snowstorm. As usual. Jackie's two daughters, her best friend and her grand-daughter slipped and slid down to the Bow, snow in our shoes, our noses red and running. The day before it had been summer. Now the water was black and the sky low with grey clouds.

We scattered the last of her ashes on the riverbank, into the river, and, after a particularly familiar gust of wind, onto our trousers. An earnest pair of mallards came to investigate the offerings.

After sampling some ash, they abstained for the rest of our brief, simple ceremony. When we were done we tried to shoo them away, but they refused to return to the water. They waddled up the steep bank, struggling over snow and rocks; they came along behind us on the path.

My mother had been right, as she often was: I carried her inside me now as she had once carried me. On the riverbank in her least favourite weather, I could hear her say, "Poor things. It's bloody freezing out. Why the hell aren't they flying south?" When we began to cross busy Memorial Drive, we were afraid they would follow us into the traffic. As though on cue, her best friend turned and said, loudly, "Why aren't you flying south?" But they remained on the curb, looking as crestfallen as a pair of ducks can look. My mother would have felt for them, their hunger, their webbed feet splayed in the abrupt snow. They quacked and quacked as we walked away.

The Stones of the Ancestors

Gorčin Dizdar

The mountains of central Bosnia are covered in a carpet of lush green meadows, pierced sporadically by amorphous fragments of protruding, barren rocks. Upon closer observation the rocks reveal their intriguing shapes, imposing a quiet presence upon the sensually overwhelming vegetation. A very few finally appear molded by a consciousness: the *stećak*, the graves of the ancestors. The engravings on their surfaces are fading: letters metamorphosed into the lightest shades of disconnected lines, symbols disfigured to inexplicable fragments of dumb matter. Only a passage of time reveals a lasting vitality: a subtle game of light and stone commences at dawn and draws to a close at sunset, as fragments of stories come to life through the sliding angle of the falling rays of light.

Drawn to this fragile phantasm of death, light and meaning, one is forced to discuss and debate, to dig out the ancient bones, to judge their sins anew. Ignored is their oft-repeated inscription— "do not touch into my bones"—reduced to a naïf "remnant of pagan beliefs" or, worse, a mere repetition of exclamations made by the distant, unknown Subject of History. The truth machinery gallantly rides in, equipped with a "sophisticated" theory or, better yet, with a non-committed interdisciplinarity that has, behind curtains, confessed its incurable narcissism …

There's a video on Youtube of Derrida being interviewed by an American journalist. "Love," she asks, "what do you think about love?" Derrida is dumbstruck, hesitates, tries to say something, then responds, emphatically, "You can't ask me *that.*" On a second clip he justifies his reaction, claiming it was very *American* of the journalist to pose such a question. When he first visited the US, Derrida continues, he was surprised that in academic and social situations the Americans tend to ask: "Can you elaborate on that?" The question appears inappropriate in France, where there is no such thing as *mere elaboration.* But the timeless, seductive subject shouts "truth"; he has no notion that he is like a light directed at my naked skin and my bones. The subject shouts "truth" and who am I to question the subject—so here, I will give you my truth.

'Twas a long time ago—some say the year was 900 AD or thereabouts—there appeared in the lands of the Bulgarian Empire a certain Bogomil, whose name means "dear to God," preaching the dangerous doctrine of apostolic poverty and Satan's dominion over the Earth, telling the people that bread is bread and water is water, but the Word is God. How many names were not given to them?—heretics and Bogomils, Paterens and Cathars, Babuns and Massaliani—grand words debated in the cells of those striving to destroy the evil in their bodies and this world, so that the Mother Church may reign supreme. The word, so the story goes, spread like wildfire through Bulgaria, Serbia, Bosnia, Italy, Germany and France … Some dare to see the Reformation as one of its branches mutated almost beyond recognition. Rare voices point to the continuities between the burning heretics and the burning witches. Yet all these attempts will remain an exotic vanguard as long as the questionable rupture between the "late Middle Ages" and "the early modern period" remains deeply entrenched—not so much in what professional historians say, as in the extent to which a certain meta-discourse of Western civilization is continually perpetuated.

Due to the density of conflicting discourses in which it is included as a signified, the *stećak* reveals the discrepancy between mutually opposed interpretations of "raw historical facts" with particular clarity. The borders around this object of historiography are initially drawn spatially and temporally. A number of around 65 000 stones is customarily given, thus providing spatial limitations roughly corresponding to the borders of the Bosnian kingdom in the fourteenth century. Certain estimations are usually added, suggesting that the number of stones may have been twice as high in the nineteenth century. Then they are classified as "medieval," dated between the twelfth and sixteenth century, when their production ceases after the arrival of the Ottoman Empire. But can we assume such a stable connection between space and meaning? Are we not making a fatal mistake in deciding to look only at the stones? Is the border between the "inside" and the "outside" of this object a rupture? Upon closer examination the temporal limit appears equally hasty—does the *stećak* truly disappear? Many of its elements can be found on Islamic, Christian and Jewish monuments of later centuries: to speak of the disappearance of the *stećak* is to speak of a gradual displacement rather than a sudden disappearance.

One of the most common motifs found on the *stećak* stone is the stag, often hunted by men and hounds, occasionally illuminated by rosettes in his antlers. In central Asian mythography the world is divided into the masculine, paternal underworld of fire and the feminine, maternal sky of water. The deer is a celestial animal, eternally descending into the underworld to carry off the sun into the sky, only to be ruthlessly hunted down again. Thus the stag is a transgressor, an intermediary between two realms within which human existence—or existence in general—unfolds. He is a figure of circular, subversive movement.

Immediately a *Christian* meaning comes to mind … but what do we know about Christianity, whereby I mean not only the "we" of the academic community, but the "we" as a disjointed, postmodern collection of individuals or, better still, "intersection of discourses"? A multitude of disparate institutions, ranging from deeply entrenched national, imperial or multinational corporations to marginal appearances such as the *Iglesia Maradoniana* (counting a respectable 100 000 members according to wikipedia) are laying claim to be the true interpreters of the Word of God. What do they say about the Christian meaning of the stag? Who wrote the books? Who painted the paintings?

Where is it then, the meaning, I mean, of the deer? In a book? In a mind? In the stone? Where is meaning? Faced by this methodological problem, by the sand of history gliding through one's fingers, the temptation arises to abandon the futile quest for "truth," to remain content with observing the dumb surviving fragments, to reflect upon their coexistence with and gradual merging into the surrounding environment.

But on it pushes, a "disinterested curiosity" imposing further elaboration, for the story is disjointed, the singular moments of insight insufficient. Ruptured along and across, the tormented homeland calls out for a signifier, something to speak about so the dead may be forgotten. The mighty Astro-Hungarian Empire, to which my country was allocated at the 1878 Berlin Congress, first dared to upset the dead, setting up a representative collection of gravestones—*stećak* on one side, Roman headstones on the other—in front of the newly built National Museum.

Strangely, it was not until I had become acquainted with issues of post-colonialism that I came to pay attention to the fact that no Muslim (or, for that matter, Catholic, Orthodox or Jewish) gravestones were included in this venerable gallery of ancestors. The Austro-Hungarian administration was focused on promoting its idea of a Bosniak identity, working hard to suppress the dissident voices among the country's religious groups, ignorant still of the outrageous hypothesis of the return of the unconscious soon to be developed in its capital. In Stolac, a town in the south of the country, the Empire built a road right through the middle of the most famous *stećak* necropolis in the country, containing the largest number of engraved stones, destroying an unknown number in the process.

The Radimlja necropolis is located on the outskirts of Stolac in an environment deeply contaminated by layers of historical and contemporary significance, the disciplinary divisions inevitably collapsing. On top of a hill barely one kilometre from the necropolis lie the ruins of Daorson, the largest known town of the Balkan's pre-Slavic inhabitants, the Illyrians. In its immediate vicinity one can see the typical burial mounds of the Illyrians, onto which *stećak* stones were grafted in numerous other locations. Closer still, almost merging with the necropolis, the Roma, the untouchables of the Balkans, have set up camp, waiting for a distant institution to decide their fate, waiting for the anthropologist to "give them a voice," so that more books may be written and more words may be wasted. A flag of Herceg-Bosna, the pseudo-republic created by the Herzegovinian Croats in 1993, only to be dismantled a year later, reminds of another story to be told, the story of the destruction of the town's architectural heritage, the fifteen-century mosques and the nineteenth-century cinemas, a vicious attack on the professed values of "Western civilization," carried out, paradoxically, in the name of that very same civilization. On the other side, a newly constructed monument, devoted to the victims of Bleiburg, the tens—some say hundreds—of thousands of Croat civilians associated with the fascist World War II regime, captured by the British and executed by Tito's Partisans on the Austrian-Slovenian border in 1945 ... The "truth" of this event remains contested and hidden, the monument's location creating another layer of significance, another intricate, opaque knot in this region's volatile historical consciousness.

Finally, the unmistakable, violent presence of Capital: monstrous machinery digging out sand, diverting the course of the stream that has given the name to the necropolis ... On the other side, the signs of consumerism in its Balkanian, unsophisticated guise: a large structure, tacked together from aggressively cheap materials, serving as a car wash facility. Built during the 1990s war, it may have originally served the bourgeoning market of stolen cars, the largest of its kind in former Yugoslavia, set up only a few kilometres away due to the town's proximity to the three warring sides. Such is the grotesque environment in which the most famous collection of the fifteenth-century Bosnian-Herzegovinian sculptures continues its unassuming existence.

But what happens to the stag at night, down in the scorching environment of the underworld, where the sun lies dormant and safely tucked away? How does he succeed in liberating himself from the stern world of the Father? Why is he allowed to steal the Father's fire? The transgressor reveals his dual nature, his secret pleasure forever hidden from view. Thus we pray that our stones may forever remain part of the environment, never to be cleansed, whitened and fenced off, turned into a signifier of another narrative, a product to be displayed and sold. No. We pray for their sincerity, so that we may always be aware of the now in which they exist.

Forgive me, O Reader, if you find no sense in my story. I have tried to show you the bones of my ancestors, but all I have found was the barren soil underneath their withering gravestones.

The Approaches

Robert Finley

None of it has anything to do with us, except for the few things we have brought with us: the faint outline of the sails against a starless sky, the contours of the hull where wave foam inscribes it, the compass with its lick of flame, like a locket opened. And there is also the tentative narrative of our arrival here, a story the navigator has plotted from day to day from the day of our departure. We appeared on this chart an hour ago, about half way down the right-hand margin, and an inch or two in from it, a small X at the end point of a ruled line in pencil. This is where we begin. A white sheet of paper, heavy, creased from folding, about a yard square, stained here and there with rust or coffee, blued slightly at the upper-left corner. A chart of nothing we have a name for: not of a bay behind a headland, not of a reach or gut or arm, not of a body of water, but of water itself, an element on the move, moon slung, pure sea sway. The depth is marked in fathoms. It is 2:30 in the morning, and the darkness goes down a long way. It will be grey dawn before we cross over the braided margin and onto the next chart, where the land appears: the Harbour and Approaches.

Thin light comes up, thumbed into the fog all around us, and reveals nothing but ourselves and the boat-length horizon that contains us. We pick up the lightship on the radio-direction finder, its signal suddenly appearing out of a static of rain and sea wrack. And then in a chorus of call and answer its ship's horn sounds from far off: first the coded signal from the radio down below,—.—, then, faint at first, below hearing, the heavy sound of the horn itself moving the heavy air. We lift across the grain of the groundswell, the wind in the southwest, and gradually the gap between them closes as we close the distance between us and the weed-heavy ship with its high tower we never see, its blind light, its sleeping crew.

I have three guides in this, each with a rope of names made of sea-crossings plied together: Finley, Angus, Allen, Cassells, Stuart, Arsenault, Martin, Mack, Townsend, Fosseler, Ferguson, Mühlig, Pyman, Tempest, Tardy, Ware … One is bent over the chart, his hands light on the woven surface, each incremental minute of latitude a taut string that sounds differently, a slow mile; one is braced down below against the waves' motion and proffers hot coffee with rum in a yellow mug, and, in the same hand held up over the threshold of the companion way, a biscuit clasped between her first and middle fingers; one is at the wheel—rain and spray stream down the brim of his foul-weather gear hood as he reaches forward. All of them pale with sleeplessness, and cleansed by it, and by the sea sound rocked, emptied of everything. Coming in.

Coming into harbour. I suppose I see them now at a little distance, sitting here at this window in this city in the rain. But I am *in* this picture too, as is my brother, tiny, alert to the slackening wind and easing motion. We are buttoned into orange foul-weather gear, cold, and eager for the mnemonic scent of spruce, crowberry, fir, juniper, that will in a moment slide down off the headlands and over us like a benediction, or like a word for home. By mid-afternoon we come in under Chebucto Head, its looming presence, its mass and height marked out for us in the fog only by the sound of the surf and by the diaphone that booms and sighs far above us, its voice full of warning and of welcome and of something, in its shifting note, a sadness more than simply human—and then again, twice on every moment. We alter course just east of north to run down the harbour's western shore. The wind drops to nothing, and the groundswell swings around behind us and lifts us in, one wave after the other, an awkward bundle passed from hand to hand along the granite wall behind its stone grey curtain.

This is where the place names start with their stories of panic or of plenty: Portuguese Cove, Bear Cove, Halibut Bay, Hangman's Beach, Neverfail, Herring Cove, Mars Rock, Ferguson's Cove … And with them the first small sounds, with their pressing intimacy, are carried out to us through the sound-amplifying fog. They are the ordinary sounds of community life and seem momentous, heart-breaking, true against the day and night and day of sea surf, our listening tuned already to a different scale in this short time at sea as though we were arriving from a far-off place and for the first time upon this shore. The low voices of mackerel fishermen balanced at the end of the gap-toothed pier are suddenly near at hand; a car door opens somewhere behind the banked fog, and then closes, and then a soft exchange of voices, easy, understated, trailing off—something about a key betraying a casual intercourse, lives locked into a day, a hand that touches the side of a face as it smooths a damp strand of hair back into place.

Here the harbour narrows and divides. Granite turns to ironstone beneath the hull. Beneath the pendulum of the keel, dismembered hulks play out the rhythm of their construction in reverse, nail after nail loosens and falls out, rivets calcify, blister, dissolve to salt; a fluted point once carried back from the far highlands lies where it was unwrapped and dropped and clicked and broke its edge against a hearthstone; beside it a bicycle that stands upright on an ancient riverbank; beneath the hull, beneath the seethe and settling of the city's effluent, pollen whispers through an ancient hemlock grove among old tires, bottles, shoes, and broken plates. We feel our way in blind.

Coming into harbour thus, under a lowering sky, the place itself obscured by fog and rain, and now by the darkening late afternoon, where is it they are coming into, my three guides who bring me with them? The ring of rigging on moored boats, hammer beats, roadwork, a flatbed backing up, all passed by unseen, their measure slowed by the fog they sound through, and yet drawing in the mind's eye the contours of a known shoreline, the crosshatched streets that rise behind it. Just as the sound of falling rain might wake a sleeper in a city late on a summer afternoon to trace the shape of things beyond the shadowed room—the sound of rain on the roof, the sound of rain on leaves, and farther off rain that pools and splashes onto stone, rain on water—just the same, the sounds of the city come breaking in on us and lead us in. And there are other sounds that come along with these, and to which, I know, we are orienting ourselves: the sound of voices mostly, the babble of any port that carries out across the water and dissolves. But for us there are among them the soft-voiced cook, the nurse, the social worker, three sisters who made their own way; also the novice who threw his books in the sea and suffered a sea change; the school principal struck down by a street car; two girls, one dancing, one kneeling neatly upon her knees; a child lost, oh the loss the loss, a secret kept; also the gambler; the good man; the gardener with his famous coronet; the father full of laughter and of tricks; the great and tragic beauty in her Dublin shoes, her cases packed, time already gone on ahead; there is the tailor; the builder; the joiner; the sailor; the teacher late for school one day in December, who stood up, her pale skin unscathed, and shook out her glass-torn cape in a ruined place; the girl full of promise who left, with her braided hair, only the lovely plain garland of her name; also there is the sound of fingers that move lightly over shoals of braille, others shaping words out of the shapes of air around them. These lead us in.

A lifetime is not long in a place, in the scheme of things, it's true, nor is a century or two or three measured against the place itself, or against the claims of others. But it is something, after all, and is passed from hand to hand, and into mine. As evening falls, we come in under the loom and the lee of the land, and pick up our mooring line in the oil-iridescent calm. We pack our gear and make our way to shore, in the tightrope dinghy overloaded, and take in the strangeness of the solid earth beneath our feet, the speed and order of the drive home along the lit city streets. But this first night back on land, and at sea in a bed that seems too large and still, not bunked in the close cabin but alone in a room that is too straight and square and empty of the chorus of our breathing, I am at first too light to sleep, a child adrift amidst the heavy furniture passed down. And when I do it is to rock all night beyond the shoals of stars.

Sometime before dawn the rain starts up again, drumming on the window, roof and eaves. My lips taste salt and burn. City, stone vessel on the edge of things, hull lifting on the thrumming tide, carry me.

A Tangle of Rainbows: The Quartet for the End of Time

Eric Friesen

God has not been entirely silent through the horror of the past 100 years, although one could be forgiven for thinking so. Just when it seemed that Hitler's Third Reich would triumph across Europe, a young French composer stared down the apocalypse with nothing but his faith, his talent, and his vision for another future. The result is a hauntingly beautiful, otherworldly master-piece of twentieth-century chamber music: *The Quartet for the End of Time* (Quatuor pour la fin du Temps) by Olivier Messiaen.

Messiaen was already a noted avant-garde composer, teacher, and star organist in Paris, when, at the beginning of the Second World War, he was conscripted into the French army as a medical orderly. In May of 1940, as the German Panzer divisions were slic-ing through Allied defences and the French army was being routed, Messiaen was captured near Nancy and sent to a prisoner-of-war camp, Stalag VIIIA in the vicinity of Görlitz, Silesia (now Zgorz-elec, Poland). The spirits of Messiaen and his fellow prisoners were very low. Not only were they confined under harsh conditions, but these proud Frenchman were having to cope with the capitulation of Paris and northern France to the Reich and the installation of the Vichy regime to the south. There was a glint of silver lining, however, in that the German army officers in charge of Stalag VIIIA were not particularly sympathetic to the Nazi leadership. As word spread that a distinguished French composer was in their midst, the camp administration allowed him some special privi-leges. Thanks to a music-loving and sympathetic guard, Messiaen soon acquired music paper, pencils, and an eraser, was relieved of other duties and given an empty barracks in which to compose without being disturbed. Within months he produced an eight-movement quartet for the unusual combination of violin, cello, clarinet, and piano, his choice of instrumentation being strictly limited by the players available in the camp. With him in Stalag VIIIA were three other captured French soldiers who happened to be musicians: cellist Étienne Pasquier, violinist Jean le Boulaire, and an Algerian Jewish clarinetist, Henri Akoka.

On a bitterly cold evening in January 1941, Messiaen's *Quartet* had its premiere in unheated Barrack 27, its windows thick with frost, and snow drifting in through the gaps in the door. The concert had been promoted by a handdrawn poster in Art Nouveau style, with the camp's stamp of approval (*Stalag VIIIA 49 geprüft*) on it. Some 300–400 prisoners, including POWs on stretchers and those from the quarantine section, crowded into this unlikely concert space, with many of the camp's German officers shivering to attention in the front row. The temperature inside was barely above freezing, the only heat generated by the accumulated bodies. Instead of concert dress, Messiaen and his fellow musicians wore tattered Czech army jackets and oversized wooden clogs.

What this odd collection of captives and captors heard on that freezing Silesian winter's evening was music that both responded to a desperate time in Europe and transcended it. It was inspired by Messiaen's fervent, mystical Catholic faith, his lifelong love and study of birdsong, and his unusual rhythmic concoctions. On the score, Messiaen quoted from the Bible's final book, the apocalyptic Revelation, excerpts from Chapter 10, verses 1–7.

And I saw another mighty angel come down from heaven, clothed in a cloud: and a rainbow was upon his head, and his face was as it were the sun, and his feet as pillars of fire … He set his right foot upon the sea and his left on the earth … and, standing upon the sea and upon the earth lifted up his hand to heaven and swore by Him that liveth for ever and ever … saying, *There shall be Time no longer:* but on the day of the trumpet of the seventh angel, the mystery of God shall be finished … [italics mine].

The key line for Messiaen was the declaration that "there shall be Time no longer." In those months of 1940 and 1941, the German war machine seemed unstoppable. Messiaen, like so many others in Europe's occupied countries, could not have helped feeling that he was living in end times, in an apocalyptic nightmare. But, as the *New Yorker's* Alex Ross points out, there was also a strictly technical meaning to the idea of time ending: "by 1941, this composer no longer wanted to hear time being beaten out by a drum—one, two, three, four; he had had enough of that in the war. Instead he devised rhythms that expanded, contracted, stopped in their tracks, and rolled back in symmetrical patterns," inspired by *The Rite of Spring* and the rhythmic patterns of Hindu Indian music. Messiaen would later refer to himself as "compositeur et rythmicien."

The whole and the parts of the *Quartet* are suffused with sacred meaning. Why eight movements? Messiaen wrote in his notes to the score: "Seven is the perfect number, the creation of the world in six days sanctified by the divine Sabbath. The 7th day of rest extends into eternity and becomes the 8th day of indestructible light and unchangeable peace." I love Messiaen the wordsmith almost as much as Messiaen the composer.

The *Quartet*'s opening movement, "Liturgy of Crystal," is filled with birdsong at dawn, one of Messiaen's favourite times of day. The second movement opens and ends with a jagged "Vocalise: for the Angel Announcing the End of Time," with a central section Messiaen described as "the impalpable harmonies of heaven, the piano playing soft cascades of chords." The third movement, "The Abyss of the Birds," is one of the most demanding clarinet solos ever written, desolately and harrowingly brooding on the sorrow of Time, with some relief from the composer's beloved blackbird song. After a brief dancelike interlude comes the first of Messiaen's two songs of praise (he uses the sensual French word "louange"): "Louange à l'Éternité de Jésus," a tender, reverent song of praise to Jesus in the voice of the cello. The music soars into an eloquent prayer of faith in the promise of the Word made flesh, even in the face of blitzkrieg. The sixth movement, "The Dance of Wrath for the Seven Trumpets," is a shocking contrast, with its awkward angular rhythms and catastrophic announcements. The seventh movement, "Tangle of Rainbows, for the Angel Announcing the End of Time," begins with another soliloquy for cello and piano. The clarinet eventually joins in as well with these lyrical lines occasionally interrupted by bursts of sound that Messiaen called "fiery swords, rivers of blue-orange lava," a tribute to the mighty angel of Revelation and the rainbow that covers him, "symbolizing peace and wisdom." And finally, the eighth movement is another louange, "In Praise of the Immortality of Jesus." This time it's the violin that pays tribute, singing an ethereal aria of "pure love ... of the creature become divine towards paradise." The quartet ends on soft bell-like chords in the piano, the violin gradually fading into eternity.

Whenever I listen to this music, I like to imagine that first hearing in Barrack 27. The POWs were a conscripted mixture of young Frenchmen: farmers, factory workers, priests, intellectuals, united in captivity. "Never before have I been listened to with such attention and understanding," Messiaen would later recall. "Even if these people knew nothing about music, they really understood that this was something special." This was not just another concert, it was an expression of divine imagination, giving hope and comfort to these desolate men.

In telling this story, it's important not to exaggerate the details. Later in life, Messiaen would remember some 5,000 POWs at the concert, that Pasquier's cello only had three strings, that the clarinet had its side keys warped by heat from a paraffin stove, and that the upright piano's keys would "remain lowered when depressed." Messiaen's wife would say he had written the *Quartet* locked in a latrine.

Dr Rebecca Rischin, an American clarinetist and scholar, sets the record straight in her superb and authoritative book *For the End of Time: The Story of the Messiaen Quartet.* There were only, at most, 400 men at that first concert; Barrack 27 could not have held more. As for the instruments, the piano was, as Rischin says, "sorely inadequate," but the cello definitely had four strings, and the violin and the clarinet were okay. Rischin also gives credit to the German officers in the camp and especially to the guard who was so helpful to Messiaen, Karl-Albert Brüll. Brüll turned out to be a real angel in Stalag VIIIA. In addition to providing materials and space for Messiaen to compose, this sympathetic German helped to forge exit documents so that Messiaen could leave the camp several months after the *Quartet*'s premiere. Brüll also kept a special eye on Jewish prisoners, advising them to stay in the camp where he felt they would receive better treatment than back in Vichy France.

While I am convinced that Messiaen's deep Catholic faith shaped every aspect of his *Quartet* , it must be said that his devotion to the Church had a very particular flavour. Alex Ross puts it this way: "He [Messiaen] loved God in terms that were sensual, almost sexual. Human love and divine love were not opposites, as they are for so many close readers of the Bible, but stages in an unbroken progression." Ross notes that "one undulating phrase in the final 'Louange' is marked 'avec amour.'" Mystical yes, fervent believer yes, but neither pious nor puritan.

Apart from the quality of the music itself, and its miraculous birth, the *Quartet for the End of Time* is unusual for its radiant declaration of love for God in the midst of suffering and hopelessness. Compare it to the profound sadness and looking back to another time of Richard Strauss' *Metamorphosen*, written in the final months of World War II as his beloved Munich lay devastated from Allied bombing. Rebecca Rischin concludes,

> … while many World War II-inspired works have understandably been absorbed with the problem of the *Deus Absconditus* (the absence of God), Messiaen's *Quartet* is not. The message the *Quartet* radiates is not one of despair, but, on the contrary, one of resounding affirmation.

Rischin reminds us that while Messiaen did not face extinction, as Jews did, and that although Stalag VIIIA was not a concentration camp: "still, in an environment that provoked depression and suicide among many of his fellow inmates, the source of Messiaen's inspiration is compelling."

Furthermore, contrast Messiaen's vision of end times to all those that dominate popular culture now. We live in a time obsessed by eschatological imaginings fuelled by a veritable apocalypse industry, in books, movies, video games, and on all other platforms of exploitative prophetic doom. In this miraculous and inspired *Quartet*, we find a man with nothing more than the power of his art, facing the end of history in a loving embrace of the divine.

I heard Messiaen's *Quartet* earlier this year on a beautiful spring evening in Banff, with the Gryphon Trio (violinist Annalee Patipatanakoon, pianist Jamie Parker, cellist Roman Borys) and clarinetist James Campbell. Rolston Recital Hall at the Banff Centre seemed eons away from that freezing January night in Stalag VIIIA, and yet I came away convinced that we need this music today as much as Messiaen's audience did in the darkest days of the Second World War. Happily, the Gryphon Trio's new recording of the *Quartet* with Jim Campbell has just been issued on the Analekta label, so I encourage you to listen for yourself. There is another Canadian recording, featuring the Amici Ensemble on Naxos. And then there is the classic recording of the *Quartet* by the group Tashi—with pianist Peter Serkin, cellist Fred Sherry, clarinetist Richard Stoltzman, and violinist Ida Kavafian—available at budget price on RCA Victor Gold Seal.

The Wrong Way

Sierra Skye Gemma

After the service, the five of us—Devan, Garrett, Morgan, Steele, and I—crammed into my rental car and drove to a nearby Mexican restaurant. Devan's sister, Morgan, wrapped in a black pencil skirt that matched her thin, cropped hair, stayed outside to finish her cigarette. When she came in, Steele—the youngest cousin and, strangely, the most boisterous of the bunch—was wearing one of the restaurant's mariachi hats, which otherwise served as decoration. He was being silly and we couldn't stop laughing. Neither could the waiter when he came over. Delighted by our energy, he asked, "Is it someone's birthday?"

No. No, it was not.

Morgan ordered a Coke. Devan said that Morgan was embalming herself from the inside out with Coke, booze, and cigarettes.

"It's true!" Morgan squealed and we all laughed some more. We were ridiculous. We were, somehow, high on life.

After lunch, we got into the car again. The energy had died back down.

"What next?" I asked from behind the wheel.

"Let's take a drive," Steele suggested and we took off into the back hills of Northern California.

Garrett, quiet and serious despite his tattoos and piercings, with a slow and steady type of thought and speech, observed how green the hills were. Steele, as the sole resident of those hills, shrugged. I thought it looked dry, but I was from Vancouver, one of the greenest cities in the world. Morgan and Devan, however, agreed, having also come from Southern California.

"Where am I driving?" I asked Steele.

"Well, we can drive up into the hills by where my friend lives. Anyone want weed?"

Why yes, we did.

"I'll navigate then," Steele said.

We drove for about an hour, way up into the hills. Steele told us about how one night he and his friend had walked a few miles to a grow-op in the woods, trespassed onto the property, and stolen about a pound of big, beautiful bud.

After much contemplation of my own tumultuous teenage years, I had already come to the conclusion that you can't make teenagers *do* anything. They will do what they will do, and all you can do is try to gently guide them and hope they don't get themselves killed. I think it was this philosophy that kept my relationships with my eight nephews and nieces so strong throughout their adolescence. They knew they could tell Auntie Sierra anything and I would never tell their parents, unless I seriously thought their lives were in danger. I preferred to guide them on my own, sans parental influence and the inevitable communication shutdown that came with it.

"Steele, as great as this pot is, I highly recommend that you don't trespass and steal it again. Seems really dangerous. I don't want you to die over dank, okay?"

"No worries," Steele said, "I don't know how we could ever smoke all that we already have anyway."

He directed me up a one-lane dirt road, carved into ruts by rainfall and repeated passage. I was worried about my rental car, but I didn't say anything.

"Pull over here," he said.

I pulled over and Steele hopped out. He walked off the road into the scraggly trees. A couple of minutes later, he was back with another shaggy blonde boy who also looked about fifteen. They could've been brothers. Steele's real brother, Tristan, had chosen to stay behind with the "adults," while all the "kids" had left with me. Tristan was too much of a people pleaser. I worried about him. I worried about how what had happened would change him, both of the boys, all of us, really.

Steele's friend peered into the car and waved. We waved back and smiled, trying to look like we cared about something more than the weed, but we didn't. The friend handed Steele a brown paper lunch bag and Steele got back in the car.

"Buuuuud!" he said, and the cousins mimicked him.

I thought briefly about all the laws I was breaking. I got a little sick, a nervous stomach, and ignored it, pushed my fears aside. What was important was that I help these kids feel the way I was feeling, which was truly, genuinely just fine.

In 1969, in her book, *On Death and Dying*, Elizabeth Kübler-Ross first introduced her theory, commonly known as The Five Stages of Grief. The five stages—denial, anger, bargaining, depression, and acceptance—have become so deeply embedded in our modern understanding of grief that we have forgotten that the Kübler-Ross Model was originally envisioned to explain the experience of terminally ill patients. Now the stages are used to describe not only how we react to the death of a loved one, but almost any experience of loss. Twenty-two years after publishing *On Death and Dying*, Kübler-Ross concluded, "Any natural, normal human being, when faced with any kind of loss, will go from shock all the way through acceptance."

This is how loss is done, folks.

I didn't even want a cat. I'm not a "pet person." I like pets about as often as I like people. Not that often. Sure, a pet can grow on you, just like a person can, but it takes time to develop that relationship. I don't see a small ball of fuzz and love it on sight. So, when William decided we should get cats, I was reluctant. Unfortunately, the man who became my first husband could talk me into almost anything.

We went to the Humane Society. He picked out a black cat with white socks. I thought it was overly excitable.

A little multi-coloured tabby walked over to me and nudged against my hand. I petted her and she started to purr. She sat down next to me.

"I like this one," I told William. He scowled at the cat.

"A tabby? Tabbies are boring. They're ugly. Look at this one. Isn't he cute? I'm going to call him Hobbes."

It was my turn to scowl. "Hobbes is an orange cat—an orange tabby, by the way—not black."

"Then I'll name him Calvin. Isn't that right, Calvin? Yes, it is. Would you like to come home with me and the grouchy lady? Okay," William said to the cat.

"That cat is spastic. I'm not getting that cat. I'm getting this one. It's my apartment."

"Fine, we'll each get one. I'll take care of Calvin and you can take care of that boring cat."

"Whatever," I said. The ultimate word in any relationship spat. We went home with two cats.

I named my cat Suzie. I liked Suzie, but I didn't *love* her. I respected her as another individual living in my home and I believe she respected me. She didn't go to the bathroom anywhere other than in her litter box. She didn't scratch my furniture while I was out. She didn't mew too loudly or too much. But I knew that if she got kitty leukemia, she'd be on her own. I liked her, but I wasn't about to go into debt to save her. It wasn't that kind of relationship.

Then, one day, Suzie disappeared.

At first, I thought she was just sleeping or hiding in the apartment, but as I called her name over and over, shook the bag of cat food, and opened a can of tuna—all to no avail—I realized that she was definitely not in the apartment. I ran to the balcony and looked down at the two-storey drop. Could a cat land on its feet after that drop? I didn't see her broken and bent body among the bushes. To be sure, I ran outside and scoured the slope below my balcony. No body.

Then I just lost it. I screamed her name hysterically. I begged and bargained and threatened her to show herself. I looked around buildings. I searched strangers' patios. William tried to calm me, but I became enraged.

"Don't tell *me* to calm down!" I yelled.

After about a half hour of looking for Suzie while battling a barrage of emotions, I saw her underneath a car. I called to her, but it was as though I was a stranger. She wouldn't come. I tried to grab her and she fought and hissed. She scratched me until I let go, and then she ran. William and I gave chase and finally cornered her. I got a hold of her leg and wouldn't let go until I finally had her secured. When we got her into the house, I started crying and couldn't stop.

Between sobs I said, "I didn't think I cared. I didn't think I cared so much."

In her article, "New Ways to Think about Grief," Ruth Davis Konigsberg makes the argument that Kübler-Ross broke the "stoic silence that had surrounded death" since the First World War. Konigsberg believes that the twentieth-century evolution from a religious model of grief to the new (North) "American Way of Grief" was the direct result of Kübler-Ross's seminal work. In less than half a century, grief had developed from an emotion to a "process" that an individual had to "work" through. Rituals of the past had been traded in for new rituals, such as grief counselling, journaling, "talking it out" with friends and family. Konigsberg points out the insidious nature of the new rules of grief: "So while conventions for *mourning*, such as wearing black armbands or using black-bordered stationery, have all but disappeared, they have been replaced by conventions for *grief*, which are arguably more restrictive in that they dictate not what a person wears or does in public but his or her emotional state" (emphasis mine).

This is how you *feel* loss.

I hadn't called my sister in three months. She'd left several messages that I hadn't returned. Since her "accident," it was hard to talk to her. She was getting better, but it was still a struggle.

The accident wasn't really an accident. She'd overdosed yet again, but this time had been the worst. Her boyfriend had found her unresponsive, with green froth foaming from her lips. The ambulance came. Her blood oxygen level registered 45%.

"That's the lowest our machine goes," the EMT had said.

The ICU nurses had warned us that brain damage was probable, but we paid no heed. April would come out of it because she was a survivor. Then she mistook the remote control for the phone. Then she couldn't dress herself. It was downhill from there.

After weeks in the hospital, my mother had finally taken April into her own custody. Our mother hadn't been able to locate a suitable institution. When I first called, April had been emotionless, almost inanimate.

"Hello? Who is it?" I said when my mother gave April the phone. I said it in the funny accent like the French castle guard in *Monty Python and the Holy Grail.* That's how we'd always said hello. There was no reply. Then I asked, "April, can you hear me?"

"Yes."

And that was pretty much how the rest had gone. Only one-word replies to direct questions. Nothing more.

But slowly, after months, April started to change. She could hold short conversations. I remember the first time we laughed together. I said, "Hey! You laughed!"

"Yes, but I'm not as funny as I used to be," she said.

"Well, you are still funny."

"But not like before."

That was now months ago. What she'd said had been true. She just wasn't as funny anymore and it was hard to talk to her. I knew I'd pushed my delay to return her call as long as I possibly could and I finally called back. No one picked up. I left a message.

The next day I prepared a package for her. The most recent

journal I had edited. A letter announcing an award I had won at school. A print-out of my most recent grades.

I wanted her to be proud of me, if that was possible.

The next week, my mother called.

Casey, my second husband, looked at the caller ID.

"It's your mom."

My mother never called me. Unless there was a tragedy to share.

"Oh God, someone is probably dead," I told Casey. "I hope it's my dad and not my sister."

But the call was about my sister. She'd had another overdose on the day I had left my message. She'd been in the ICU the last week, and our mother had been at her side ever since, unable to call me back. Or whatever.

"I don't even know where she got the drugs," my mother cried.

I had to contact my older brother Dane, since my mom didn't talk to him either. Not even for tragedies.

He was in Japan. I emailed him to call me as soon as possible. I said it was an emergency.

"Do you know what time it is here?" he asked, irritated, when he called. "It's three a.m. What's the big emergency?"

"It's April. She's in the ICU. She tried to commit suicide again. Pretty serious this time. She left a note."

Dane sighed. "You know, she had so much potential when she was younger, but she just failed at everything. I mean, she even failed at killing herself."

April started healing. Mother called and said she was doing better. She'd had a little Jell-O. So, it was quite a shock when she died suddenly a few days later. It was quite a shock for everyone but me.

Kübler-Ross didn't believe that the stages always came in the same order for all people. Some people skipped stages or got stuck and never progressed. Others bounced back and forth between two stages or roller-coastered through three or four stages again and again, as if they were on a never-ending track. Despite these variations, she believed that all individuals experienced at least two of the stages in their grieving process.

When my son Liam was about five years old, I thought it would be a great experience for him to have an aquarium. So, we went to the store, and on the suggestion of the employee there, came home with a small fish tank, all the fancy little decorative displays, rocks, a beta fish, and an aquatic frog. My son named the two "Fishy" and "Froggy," respectively.

From day one, Fishy seemed to have quite the personality, for a fish. Froggy, while absolutely adorable with his little webbed feet, wasn't thriving as Fishy was. He swam little and didn't seem to like any of the three brands of frog food that we bought. With each day, he was swimming around less and less and just hanging out at the bottom of the tank more and more.

That's okay, I thought, if Froggy dies, he will float to the surface and I'll know right away that he has passed on.

A few days later my in-laws, with whom we lived at the time, mentioned that Froggy hadn't been moving much the past few days, *at all*. As I walked over to the tank, I assured myself that Froggy was still alive because dead fish, and presumably all aquatic beings, float to the surface when they die. Right? I bent down and squinted into the tank. I was met with glazed-over gray eyes. I took a deep breath and stood up.

"That's okay," I said to my son's grandmother Shannon. "I'll have to … I'll have to … I don't know what to do!"

As the idea of removing Froggy's remains from the tank and the thought that the beta fish was swimming around in *dead frog water* sunk in, I started to panic. I was nearly hyperventilating as I tried to work out what to do.

I turned to Shannon, a nurse of fifteen years, "Shannon, I'm not used to this. I thought I could handle this, but I can't. You're used to death Shannon, can you take care of it? I just don't think I can do it," I whined. "I don't know what to do. What will I say to Liam?! Maybe he won't notice. Maybe we can just flush the frog and he'll never even notice. Oh God, I can't do this right now. I need some time to think. I'm going to go take a shower and then I'll think about it."

As I walked to my bathroom, I heard Shannon laughing at me and then calling Liam in to tell him that Froggy was no more.

While I stood under the cleansing waters of the hot shower, I thought of John Updike's 1969 poem "Dog's Death." The poem is about a family pet, whose life is cut short just as she is "beginning to learn / To use the newspapers spread on the kitchen floor / And to win, wetting there, the words, 'Good dog! Good dog!'" Never having had a natural affinity with the fauna of the Pacific West Coast, I surprised myself with tears every time I read the final stanza:

> Back home, we found that in the night her frame,
> Drawing near to dissolution, had endured the shame
> Of diarrhea and had dragged across the floor
> To a newspaper carelessly left there. Good dog.

In the shower, I was thinking about writing my own poem that showcased, by the death of Froggy, my many failures as a mother.

As I was structuring the poem in my mind, I heard a little knock at the bathroom door.

"Come in," I said, and I heard my son enter.

"Mommy?" he said, "I have something to show you."

My breath caught in my throat and I knew that my son was about to confront me with the terrible truth that I had never known how to care for any sort of aquatic animal. What had I been thinking? With fear, I pulled back the shower curtain, ready to face the worst.

"See?" my son said, with his hand outstretched.

"Mmm," I said, "a cookie."

Later, Shannon told me that they had a short memorial service for Froggy at the toilet, just before they flushed him to Froggy Heaven. Liam hadn't reacted visibly or otherwise to the service. And my son never again mentioned Froggy, or his death, to me.

The Kübler-Ross grief process has been compared to the Schopenhauer learning process. Arthur Schopenhauer said, "All truth passes through three stages. First, it is ridiculed. Second, it is violently opposed. Third, it is accepted as being self-evident." Applying the Kübler-Ross stages to this model means associating denial with ridicule, anger and bargaining with opposition, and depression and acceptance with accepting the truth as self-evident. Reimagining Kübler-Ross's model in this way is supposed to simplify it, but it still funnels reactions into specified stages.

Dane said that when he told our oldest brother, Shawn, about April's death, Shawn had become extremely angry and had yelled, "How could this have happened?"

I laughed. I couldn't help it. Dane didn't say anything on the other end of the line.

"Um, well, a lifetime of drug and alcohol abuse?"

"I just can't believe it," Dane said.

He couldn't see my frown. "I don't understand. She's done this so many times. How can you be surprised?"

"Yeah, but she always survived. She always pulled through. I thought this would be like every other time."

"Well, you had to know," I said, "that someday she'd get it right. You *had* to know."

"No. I never thought," he trailed off.

"Are you going to the funeral?" I asked.

He said he couldn't, but I thought that he just couldn't bring himself to do it.

When my mother called to tell me when and where the service would take place, she started crying. She told me how she'd left for one week—just one week!—to attend a Jehovah's Witness convention in Southern California. She thought April would be okay. April had really improved, she said. She didn't know April was doing drugs again. When she'd left, she'd told April that she only needed her to do one thing while she was gone—just one thing! She'd asked April to water the plants. When she'd come back, all the plants were dead. She was so angry, she said. She'd asked April, "Why couldn't you just do this one thing for me?"

Two days later, she found April on the floor. She said April had already turned blue.

"If only I hadn't been so hard on her. You know? About the plants?"

"That's ridiculous," I said. But then I thought, What if I had just called sooner? I immediately shook my head. No, that was silly. That was crazy talk. It wouldn't have changed anything. Not one thing. My sister had always had a death wish.

Grief counsellors have expanded the Kübler-Ross model to include seven stages:
  1)Shock or Disbelief
  2)Denial
  3)Bargaining
  4)Guilt
  5)Anger
  6)Depression
  7)Acceptance or Hope

I'm unclear as to how stage one (shock or disbelief) is radically different from stage two (denial). Don't disbelief and denial go hand in hand?

What do I know? I'm no expert.

Some experts have also pointed out that the "grief-cycle" may not be limited to merely emotional "side effects." Associated physical and social symptoms may take the form of insomnia, loss of appetite, self-imposed social isolation, and difficulty functioning at home, school, or work.

The day after my sister died, I walked into the student lounge of the History department. All my friends from the department were there. As one, their faces turned towards me. Surprise. Shock. Eyes widened to exactly the same degree. Mouths ever so slightly agape.

"Why are you here?" Isabel asked.

"I have class."

They continued to stare.

"I have class," I repeated. What was I doing wrong? My sister wasn't going to be less dead if I skipped my classes. Plus, I had assignments due. A midterm coming up.

They all rushed me at once. Encased me in their arms.

"We're so sorry," they wailed.

Why? I wondered. They didn't know my sister. They didn't know how long she had suffered.

In 2007, the *Journal of the American Medical Association* published "An Empirical Examination of the Stage Theory of Grief," which reported the results of the three-year Yale Bereavement Study (YBS). Using Selby Jacobs' hybrid theory of grief that synthesized Kübler-Ross' stages with those identified by several other researchers, the study followed 233 participants whose family members died of natural causes. The authors hoped to determine whether the specific pattern of stages of bereavement was "normal or not." They excluded participants whose loved one died from unnatural causes (like accidents and suicides) and subjects were excluded if they appeared to meet the criteria of complicated grief disorder, "so that the results would represent normal bereavement reactions."

As noted by other grief experts, the study was based on the *assumption* of stages of grief. The article opens with: "The notion that a natural psychological response to loss involves an orderly progression through distinct stages of bereavement has been widely accepted by clinicians and the general public." At no point in the article do the authors question these assumptions. Rather, they seek to find patterns of "normal" grief that they already believe to exist.

Jacobs' hypothesized stage theory of grief includes disbelief (or numbness), separation distress (identified as yearning, anger, or anxiety), depression-mourning, and recovery. However, the YBS specifically questioned participants regarding disbelief, yearning, anger, depression, and acceptance. Finding what they hoped to find, the YBS reported that "the 5 grief indicators achieved their respective maximum values in the sequence ... predicted by the stage theory of grief." However, just one page later, they note that "in terms of absolute frequency, and counter to the stage theory, disbelief was not the initial, dominant grief indicator. Acceptance was the most often endorsed item. Evidently, a high degree of acceptance, even in the initial month postloss, is the norm in the case of natural deaths."

How am I *supposed* to feel again?

It was my first creative nonfiction class in my first week of courses at the University of British Columbia. After years of doing what I thought was practical, I had applied to the Master of Fine Arts Program in Creative Writing. I got in.

I was elated. I was going to be a nonfiction author.

In that first class, about twenty minutes were set aside to discuss the Perils of Nonfiction. All the horror stories about everyone who had ever written a memoir and been burned. An heiress to a fortune disinherited. A reputation ruined. A relationship destroyed. Then our instructor said, "As for myself, I decided to wait for my father to die before publishing my memoirs."

I nodded. That's what I'm going to do too, I thought.

The following morning, my phone rang. The caller ID said it was my brother Dane. We hadn't spoken in two years. I thought, This can't be good.

I didn't pick up. I waited 'til he left a message so I could see what he wanted before I replied. His message only asked me to call him back.

When I called him back, he said, "I don't know how you are going to take this, but Dad is dead. He died this morning."

I had the urge to laugh, to start laughing and never stop. To laugh with my whole body. But I swallowed it down. I didn't want to offend the brother who felt no qualms about offending me.

"Oh?" was all I could manage.

Then he told me the whole story about my dad and his worsening illness and his refusal to go to a hospital and how they found him sprawled on dirty sheets in his double-wide trailer.

"I understand that you may not feel ... much, about this," Dane said.

"No, I guess, if anything, I feel ever so slightly relieved."

Then Dane got choked up. My steel-hearted lawyer brother who'd had—at best—a complicated and painful relationship with our father, started to cry. He tried to explain himself, "Now that he's dead, there is no chance it will ever be better, you know?"

"It was never going to be better, Dane."

When I hung up, I told Casey, "My dad died today. What are the chances? Yesterday, I was thinking about how I was gonna wait 'til he died to write that story, and he died *the next fucking day!*" Then I laughed.

The funny thing about being a "grief expert" is that your expertise is not in any way related to the depth or frequency of your own experience of loss. In fact, you can be an expert in grief without having grieved at all. As long as you've watched enough people do it, you're good. If this is indeed what makes an expert, then Russell Friedman and John W. James are two of the top professionals in their field. These "professional grief recovery specialists" have co-authored three books on loss and have worked with over 100,000 grieving people during the past three decades.

"The Myth of the Stages of Dying, Death, and Grief" argues that more harm than good has come of Kübler-Ross' theory. Damage is caused to grievers when they "try to fit their emotions into non-existent stages." I wonder, instead, about the witnesses—the friends, lovers, bystanders, co-workers—who try to fit the responses of people who have experienced a loss into these non-existent stages. The witnesses who want them to conform, to see them feel the way they think they should feel.

I think these two are on to something. Friedman and James were the first to point out that since the premise of the YBS study was flawed, so too were the results. They also argued that "since Kübler-Ross' feelings were processed through the filter of her life-long unresolved grief and retained anger," so too were her responses to those she interviewed, as well as the conclusions she drew from her research. Friedman and James highlight the fact that "in the final chapter [of Kübler-Ross' last book], titled *My Own Grief,* she tells the gruesome story about an episode involving her father and a cherished childhood pet that caused her to make an oath never to cry again. That event, along with a host of other personal grief incidents, resulted in her bottling up a lifetime of anger that she admitted she didn't deal with until very late in life." Is it any wonder then that Kübler-Ross asserted that anger was the one and only stage that *everyone* dealing with loss experienced?

But anger isn't absolute. In fact, no single grief response is. Friedman and James argue that the prevalence of the stage theory, which is so deeply rooted in North American culture, makes many patients identify with particular stages that they aren't feeling, just because that is what they think they should feel. To quote Friedman and James, for example, a typical conversation with a patient might go like this:

Patient: "I'm still in denial."

Friedman: "Do you deny that your loved one has died?"

Patient: "No."

James: "Then you are not in denial."

Similarly, grievers, and sometimes even their doctors, look for and often find a diagnosis of clinical depression, when really, they are just *sad*. And being sad, Friedman and James argue, is a pretty "normal" reaction to losing someone in your life. You know what else they think is "normal?" Whatever the griever is feeling at any point in time. Every individual feels and processes loss in their own unique way.

This is how you feel grief, folks: however you feel it.

When I was no older than twenty, I came home one day from work. My boyfriend, Chris, approached me nervously.

"Hey, your mom called."

"Oh yeah?"

"Yeah, your grandma died."

"Oh no! …Wait, which one?"

"Um, your dad's mom?" He said it like a question.

"Oh, thank God. I really like my mom's mom. Whatever, my dad's mom was a bitch."

His eyes widened in shock.

"Am I supposed to be sad that this woman died when she was only nice to me one time in her entire life? No wonder my dad's so fucked. That was the woman who raised him. She once cornered me in a room when I was about twelve and said, 'Why are you dressed like that?' Of course, my mom bought all my clothes, so I was just wearing some pretty regular shorts and a shirt. She said, 'You want the boys to look at you? You want them to look at your body?' It scared me. Then she said, 'You're gonna get raped. That's what happens to girls who dress like you. They get raped. Dressing like that is like asking for it.' I was twelve years old."

I shed no tears for her.

Some years later, my dad's dad died. He had been living in Stockton, California and once, on a road trip to Las Vegas, I thought about pulling off the road and stopping in to say hi. But I was afraid it would get around that I had been traveling to Las Vegas and I was nervous about my mom finding out about it—our relationship was tenuous at best—and having her judge me for going to the epicenter of sin was something I wanted to avoid. So I kept on driving. When he died, I had a flicker of regret that I'd never once contacted him after I had left home at fifteen.

About a year after that, my mom's dad died. She left a message on my machine. She was crying. I knew she loved him very much and I knew he'd been a good man and a loving father, but I didn't return her call. She had hurt and manipulated me too many times. I needed to protect myself. It was sad that he died, but he'd had Alzheimer's for the past few years and, anyway, he was very old—in his nineties—so it had been bound to happen soon. When I heard the message, I sat down and I wrote in my day planner, "Lloyd Matthews Parsons died today." When that year was up, and it was time to take out the old calendar pages and insert the new, I saved that page. I still have it.

Not long after my mom's father died, I was at work in my little windowless office between the Intensive Care Unit and the Cardiac Recovery Unit of Providence St. Vincent Medical Center in Portland, Oregon. There was a patient dying in the ICU. The family wanted to do everything they could to prolong their (grand)mother's life. The woman just wanted to die in peace. She kept pulling out her tubes. The nurses and the doctors talked to the family and helped them to realize that it was time and they let her go. She died surrounded by those who loved her.

I sat in my office and cried.

A nurse walked in and I tried to cover it quickly.

"You okay?" she asked.

I had a history of sharing with this particular nurse, so I told her why I was crying.

"It's weird," I said. "My own grandfather died not long ago. I cared about him. He was a sweet man. But I didn't cry. I haven't cried at the deaths of any of my grandparents. Now, someone I don't even know is dying and I can't help it: it just seems *so sad*."

"You build up those walls of yours. It's hard to let 'em down, but easier when there is no risk. What do you have to lose by mourning for someone you don't know?"

I sat stunned.

Friedman and James haven't been the only ones to counter the Kübler-Ross model of grief. George Bonanno, a professor of clinical psychology at Columbia University, shares the belief that grief does not come in stages. In fact, he finds that most people are resilient in the face of loss. His book, *The Other Side of Sadness: What the New Science of Bereavement Tells Us about Life After a Loss*, is the result of thousands of interviews over the course of two decades. He concludes that resilience is the primary reaction to grief and trauma. In other words, individuals who have suffered a loss don't necessarily even grieve. If they do not grieve, then Kübler-Ross' Five Stages of Grief lose all meaning in the face of death.

As the excitement over Steele's score settled a bit, I started driving down out of the hills. It wasn't long before one of the nephews asked who had a pipe.

"I almost brought one," Morgan said.

"I didn't even think about it," Devan said.

You, Garrett? No? Anyone? No.

They began to despair.

"Whatever," I said, "we'll just make an apple pipe."

Huh? Morgan and Steele had never heard of such a thing. Devan and Garrett had, but had never used one.

"It's easy. You just poke a few holes in an apple and you've got yourself a pipe."

They were impressed.

We drove by a little mom and pop market in the middle of nowhere. Devan, Garrett, and Morgan ran in. They found an apple and bought some Cokes and snacks that were more chemical than food—ideal for Morgan's self-embalming—but would serve the purpose when they had the munchies.

"We got an apple!" Morgan said with delight as she got back in the car.

As we started to pull out of the parking lot and back onto the road, they asked me how to make it.

"Well, we need a pen."

No one had a pen. Really? We checked the rental car's glove box. Nothing.

"Ahhhhg," I groaned. As soon as I found a place, I turned around and we headed back to the market.

"Someone go inside and ask to borrow a pen," I said.

Resistance. They couldn't do that. The cashier would *know*.

"No one is going to know anything other than we are going to ask for a pen."

Morgan went inside. The owner was in the back. She saw a used pen on the counter, grabbed it, and ran back to the car.

"Go! Go!" she said. "I stole a pen!" Her excitement was absurd, but we got a good laugh out of it anyway and I made a show of gunning the engine as I pulled back onto the road. For a moment, we were gangsters.

Steele directed us to a place we could go. "Beautiful sunsets there," he said.

I pulled in to an overlook just above the small town where Steele lived. The valley spread out before us and beyond that, more mountains. The sun was going to drip down behind those hills soon.

Devan grabbed the pen and started trying to jam it through the core. It was harder than he thought. "Here," he said, "let the expert do it."

I took the apple from him. I didn't say that I hadn't actually ever made a pipe before or that I'd only seen it done once and that was years ago. But I handled the apple like I knew what was what. I managed to get the pen through the middle, although it got stuck. I bit down on one end of the dirty pen and pulled. I looked like a pro. Then I took one small, deep bite from the skin in the middle of the apple. I spit out the cold, tart fruit with its waxy skin.

"This will be the bowl," I pointed to the bitten space. "Now I have to get a hole through the bowl down to that shaft without breaking the apple, and it can't be too big or the pot will fall through. This is a delicate business, this."

Somehow I did it. But smoking it wasn't easy. The apple's fruit was moist. It took some time to heat up the interior of the apple and get the smoke flowing. They weren't quitters though. As they struggled with the apple pipe, we chatted.

We talked about how great it was to see everyone, even if it was for April's funeral. Steele found the whole situation rather ironic. His mother had always been the one trying to keep our rag-tag team of dysfunctional family members together. It never really worked. Her death was the one thing to finally bring everyone together, well almost (Dane was still in Japan). But who knew when we'd see each other like this again? Family reunions were out of the picture, unless, maybe, someone else died.

I watched the setting sun and I thought about the last time I saw my sister. The summer before her "accident," I'd gone to visit her and Tristan and Steele at their home in Maui. Tristan was graduating from high school and April had paid for plane tickets for my son and me to visit. She had been sober for two years.

When I stepped off the airplane and sucked in that first breath of hot, humid air, I had this sinking feeling that I'd made a mistake. I pulled Liam—then six years old—close to me. Then I heard

April's characteristic excited shriek and saw her running toward me. She hugged me fiercely and I smelled the alcohol on her breath. My sister had never been sober for more than two years.

I got into the car with her. I let her chauffeur my son, her sons, and me when I knew she was intoxicated. By the time we got to the house, I was sick. I vowed never to put my son's life in danger like that again.

The next morning, I said sternly, "I'm driving for the rest of the trip." She didn't argue, and we didn't discuss why.

The next day, we drove to Wailea. As a special treat for Tristan's graduation, my sister had paid for a couple of nights at the Grand Wailea, the nicest hotel on Maui, east of Lahaina. We didn't ask how she got the money. We knew better than that.

The Grand Wailea was right on a white sand beach and had waterslides and manmade rivers and pools. It was gorgeous, but I was on edge. Our mother had arrived that morning and it was difficult to make the forced, polite conversation that our pained and broken relationship called for. April kept running off to "take care of errands." I watched over Liam, but Tristan and Steele were the perfect cousins and they, along with a few of their friends, took my little water bug on slide after joyous slide. I stood by the edge of the pool where one of the slides ended. Liam would climb the stairs to the top, wave excitedly to me, and then look for my face every time he came sliding into the wading pool. I smiled at his easy childlike bliss.

Then, something caught my eye. One of the teen girls who was friends with Tristan was talking to a security guard. They came walking towards me.

I thought, Oh no, oh no, not again.

I had been in exactly this situation before: at a hotel with my sister, a security guard comes looking for her because she's stolen another guest's six-pack of beer. She gets kicked out of the hotel.

The security guard walked up to me and asked for April. My head was swimming. I could not believe it was happening again.

"Why?" I choked out.

"Well, this young lady had her purse stolen, and she says she's here with April, so we just wanted to make sure April knew that we are doing our best to track down the thief."

I was shocked, but relieved beyond measuring. This time April was not the thief.

I ran into April as I was headed into the bathroom near the pools.

"Oh! There you are!"

Her eyes were red and glassy and I knew she had been drinking.

"Hey, I need to talk to you."

She nodded. She knew she was caught. She knew what was coming: lecture, guilt, more self-hatred that she would drink down with another bottle.

We went into the bathroom.

I stood her face-to-face with me and put my hands on her shoulders. I looked into her eyes. They started to swell with tears.

"I want you to know," I started, "that I know that you're drinking."

She nodded.

"And I also want you to know that I don't care and that I'm never going to stop loving you."

She was almost confused. She'd never heard those words before. She didn't know how to respond, what to say, so she said nothing.

Instead, she fell into my arms and sobbed and I held her for a long time, past the point where my arms started to ache and the muscles between my shoulders began to burn.

I was brought back to the hills of Northern California when one of the nephews pressed the pipe to my arm.

"We got it working. It's your turn."

"Oh no, I'm going to pass. I have to drive, remember? I have to be the responsible one." We laughed at that. How ridiculous it was to think of myself as responsible after I had contributed to the delinquency of a minor.

"Yeah," Devan said. "Aren't you supposed to be the adult here?"

"Whatever, you're all legally adults, except for Steele. I am only responsible for Steele."

"But why did you do this?" Devan continued. "No one else at that funeral would have taken us out to lunch and then on a back hills adventure to find pot."

Then I told them about the time I wanted to die. About how, living with my sister at the age of fifteen, I'd experienced my first true love and my first true heartbreak. How it feels to think your heart is going to crush and crumple until it implodes and leaves a big gaping cavity in your chest. Devan nodded his head. He was the only one who knew.

I told them about how I couldn't imagine continuing that feeling, living with that feeling, and how I wanted it to end. How when my sister had come home and found me, in a ball on my bed, sobbing and soaked through with sweat and tears, she'd told me that it would be okay and how I just needed to get through today and tomorrow would be better.

I told them how she had poured a dash of vodka and a shot of Kahlua and topped it with milk. She'd handed me the glass and a tiny pill.

"What's this?" I'd asked.

"Flexeril," she'd said, "a muscle relaxant. Down the hatch."

I had taken that pill and drunk every last drop and I'd fallen asleep and she had been right. The next day had been better.

"Sometimes," I said to the four kids before me, "the wrong thing is the right thing to do."

On the Willing Suspension of Disbelief
Wayne Grady

I: THE TRICK

A man in a tuxedo is standing before us. He shows us his hand, palm forward, palm reversed, it is completely empty; he then closes and reopens his hand: it is holding a live mouse. We think it's a trick and look for the secret fold in the tuxedo's sleeve, in the vest pocket. But there remains a doubt, or rather a belief. At a certain stage in our childhood—at a certain stage in civilization—we believed that the man produced the mouse out of thin air, out of nothing, out of darkness and dust, and a vestige of that belief lingers like an appendix. We know he did not, he could not, but then where did the damned thing come from?

In Buenos Aires, a man approaches me in a bar and asks me if I want to see some magic. I say I do. He produces a deck of cards and has me select a card from it: I choose the Queen of clubs. He tells me to write my name on the card, which I do, and he then takes a ticket-collector's punch out of his pocket, punches a hole in each of the card's four corners and tells me to replace the card in the deck. He then shuffles the deck and shakes out a card— yes, it is the Queen of clubs, only now all four holes are in one corner. I can explain everything—perhaps every card in the deck was the Queen of clubs, or he has somehow switched decks for one in which all the holes are in one corner—except for the fact that my name is still on the face of the card, exactly as I wrote it.

If I cannot bring myself to believe, even for a second, that those holes have somehow moved across the card, how can I read a novel?

II: THIS IS NOT A PIPE

A child is looking at a book. In the book are some pictures.

"What is this?" we say, pointing to one of the pictures.

"A tree," says the child.

"Very good. And this?"

"A train."

What the child is looking at is not a tree or a train, but pictures of a tree or a train. The child is learning to recognize two-dimensional representations of three-dimensional objects. But at the same time, the child is learning to see one thing and to call it something else. The child is learning not to make a distinction between illusion (a picture of a tree) and reality (a tree).

A group of American university students is given a story to read in which George Washington becomes the second president of the United States. The students have been told that what they are reading is a work of fiction. After reading the story, when the students are asked to name the first president of the United States, sixty percent of them reply that they do not know.

III: THE EXISTENCE OF MONSTERS

This spring, I opened the door of the garden shed and a mouse ran out. It was a female, and she carried her litter of six young clinging to her, each latched onto one of her teats. The weight must have been enormous, and when she stopped, panting, I saw that there was something else attached to her, a growth or protuberance emerging from her right flank. At first I thought it was a seventh offspring, but when I bent for a closer look I backed away in involuntary horror. I didn't at first know what I had seen, except that it was loathsome and alive. I had to force myself to look again. It was thick, round, hairless and segmented, like some glistening larva that had grown inside her and was tunnelling out through her side. It might have been a species of insect, but if so not any kind I had encountered before. If this thing was natural, then is the monstrous natural, evil is natural, deformed matter—Milton's hell—is natural.

A teratoma is a growth, a sort of tumour, that develops in the human body, in various locations depending on the kind of discarded cells from which it is made. Teratomas that develop from embryonal cells appear in the brain, or elsewhere in the head: in the nose, under the tongue or in the skull's sutures. Teratomas derived from germ cells turn up in the testes, in males, or in the ovaries in females. A teratomoa is a kind of trash can into which the body deposits cells it no longer needs, but which are not dead. The discarded cells continue to live and grow: teratomas have been found containing small but complete body parts, legs, arms, teeth, hair. Some have been found that contained functioning organs, an eye, for example, or a beating heart. A teratoma can grow inside a fetus, in which case it is said to be growing inside its own twin. They are the human body disconnected, disjointed, disassembled, but possibly sentient. If an eye, if a beating heart, why not a brain?

Are the monsters of fable—minotaurs, harpies, griffons, dragons, sea serpents, centaurs, mermaids, manticores, yales—simply externalized metaphors for the teratomas that subliminally we know to exist within each of us? If we think of Earth and its atmosphere as a living being, if Earth is Gaia, then Earth could produce such monsters. Caliban, offspring of the African witch Sycorax, is deformity personified, a true monster. Prospero describes him as "a freckled whelp, hag-born—not honour'd with a human shape." Human-like, having arms, legs, eyes, a beating heart and a rudimentary brain, yet not human in shape, is a fair description of a teratoma.

It was many days before I was able to approach that shed again, and when I did I was surprised to find it intact. It hadn't changed. Life went on.

IV: THE PHOTOGRAPH

A man and his wife are going through some old boxes, and a photograph falls out. It is of her, taken twenty-five years ago, before they met. In it, sunlight is streaming in from an invisible window, filling her white blouse with light, and her face, turned towards the camera, is somber and soft and reflexive. The man finds his wife beautiful now, but in the photograph her beauty is different, and not simply because she is younger. Her beauty in the photograph is one of promise, whereas her beauty now is one of fulfillment. In the photograph, it is as though she is standing at the base of a mountain looking up; now it is more as though she is at the top of the mountain looking down. His wife notices the difference, too. "I'm not the same woman I was then," she says.

The man keeps the photograph, hangs it in his study. Every time he enters the room his eyes go to it immediately, seek out her luminous blouse, her dark, tightly curled hair, her full, sensuous lips, her wide, accepting gaze. He realizes that he is falling in love with her. He almost forgets that she is his wife. He wishes he had known her then, that it had been him who took the photograph rather than a former lover. He is jealous of this man, and scornful of him for having had her and let her go. He wants to protect her from the pain of that separation, about which they have often spoken. He wants time to have stopped at the snap of the photograph, so that she will not have to go through what is to come.

He feels guilty for loving the woman in the photograph. By loving her he feels he is being unfaithful to his wife. No matter how often he tells himself that the woman in the photograph is his wife, loving her does not feel the same as loving his wife. The very act of going into his study, of closing the door and letting his eyes rest on the photograph, of experiencing the deep, thrilling calm that comes over him when he sees that she is there, still gazing openly at him from her shaft of light, is like a secret assignation, as though he and the woman in the photograph were having an affair while his wife is in the next room, reading or writing a letter or getting ready for bed.

Sometimes he manages to work in his study for hours without looking at her, he almost forgets that she is there, and when he looks up from his desk he is surprised to see her, and delighted, too, of course, as though she has turned up unexpectedly at a restaurant where he'd been dining alone. At such times he detects a hint of sadness in her eyes. She knows this can't go on, that she is destined to experience the wrench of separation, that she will be alone and then they will meet and he will not recognize her.

He takes the photograph down and lays it face-up on the windowsill—no good; he sees it every morning when he opens the curtains. He puts it in a drawer, then finds excuses to go into that drawer, to look for a pen, or an elastic band, or the night light his wife uses to read after he has gone to sleep. He thinks about taking the photograph from the drawer and returning it to the old box that was its home for the past twenty-five years, but he knows he can never do that. It would be like returning her to her former lover. He realizes he cannot now go back to simply loving his wife.

Hello, I'm Screwed

Michelle Kaeser

The meat counter at the Cambie Street Whole Foods in Vancouver is thirty feet long, filled with choice cuts of beef, lamb, chicken, pork, and at least twenty different kinds of sausages. Two clerks, dressed in white smocks, black aprons, and Whole Foods caps, hustle around behind the counter, making sure everything looks just right. One of them wraps up an antibiotic-free chicken breast; the other offers instructions on how to grill a $33/pound cut of tenderloin to a young, attentive shopper.

Philip Dunlop used to be one of these workers. From October 2009 to April 2010, he spent forty hours a week slicing meat, making sausages, and serving customers, all in workplace conditions he found increasingly depressing. The sturdy, dark-haired 30-year old recites the list: lack of respect, uneven wages, uncertain pay bumps, short staffing, inability to rectify grievances, low job security—it goes on and on. He lodged complaints about these issues to store managers in letter after letter. Each time he did, the managers spoke to him, placated him, assured him things would change. Only they didn't. Dunlop felt more and more like he was being handled—that he had no real voice in his workplace. After less than two months of working at what Dunlop calls "The Meat Pit," he started thinking about unionizing the store.

Labour in the retail sector is notoriously difficult to organize. The position of retail clerk is now the most common job in the country, at over 1.8 million workers. Yet, the field remains one of the least unionized. In Canada, nearly thirty percent of all workers are union members; less than eleven percent of workers in the retail sector are unionized. Membership is particularly low among young workers. Just under fifteen percent of those aged 15-24 are union members, half the rate of workers in any other age bracket. Even worse, labour organizers are grappling with a concerted effort among companies to change corporate culture—an insidious new way to convince workers that labour and management are playing for the same team. With such stacked odds, the future of unions in retail looks increasingly grim.

Dunlop lives in an old white house in the affluent Point Grey neighbourhood in Vancouver. It's one of the few run-down homes. He shares the space with six roommates, all of whom are students or recent graduates like Dunlop, who has a Master's degree in history. It's a February afternoon and Dunlop is making everyone sandwiches with clearance deli meat. He's dressed in old cargo pants and a much-too-large black sweater with rips along the seams, supporting his claim that he gets all of his clothes second-hand. The toonie-sized red sale sticker is conspicuous as he pulls slices of salami from the package. This is what he could afford to buy on his $11/hour wage at Whole Foods and it's the kind of meat he still buys now that he's unemployed and living off a combination of EI and meagre savings.

Dunlop was finishing up his Master's degree when he landed the job at Whole Foods in late 2009. His thesis was an exploration of the Sino-American influence on the Cambodian genocide. There wasn't much of a market for that slice of knowledge; he wound up working as a meat clerk instead. Dunlop had also studied labour history in school and had developed a sense of class consciousness. When he arrived at Whole Foods, he was both surprised and dismayed with working conditions.

Dunlop was impelled to act. He tried to build relationships with his coworkers and strengthen bonds with informal gatherings outside of the store. In conversations with his fellow employees, Dunlop suggested the possibility of alternative dynamics between labour and management. He outlined a place where workers weren't obliged to accept everything they were told without question. He was in small ways trying to break the illusion that labour and management are always playing for the same team. Months later in his kitchen, Dunlop recounts the obstacles and feelings of impossibility in between bites of the salami sandwich he's filled out with mustard, mayonnaise, tomato and a slice of Kraft singles cheese.

In January, Dunlop began to look for allies in an organizing drive. He started with his coworkers in the Meat Pit, but soon branched out into other departments, striking up conversations with grocery clerks, workers at the specialty foods counter, and a few cashiers. All of the workers he approached were under thirty. The longest any of them had been at Whole Foods was a year and a half. As Dunlop flitted about the store, he sought to get a sense of workers' attitudes toward their jobs and workplace conditions, as well as their feelings about organized labour. He was discouraged by the response. "Far from having an opinion," he says, "some didn't know what a union was."

Canada's early trade unions were established in the second half of the 19th century in response to the spread of industrial capitalism. As production accelerated in the early 20th century, so did labour activity. Escalating tensions between wealthy employers and workers facing high unemployment and inflation led to the Winnipeg General Strike in 1919, the largest general strike in Canadian labour history. In the 1930s, the Depression helped boost union appeal and by the end of World War II, workers were organized enough and militant enough to demand better wages, hours, and conditions. Strike activity surged. Unions continued to fight for rights and to gain strength, with union density (the proportion of unionized workers in the workforce) peaking in the 1980s. Since then, however, union activity has been on the decline.

Unfortunately, it's easy to see how some workers, and particularly young workers, have become less aware of unions and the role they played in shaping the 20th century. Unions aren't in the media as much as they once were—and labour news isn't exactly a hot topic on social media. There is the sense that unions are a thing of the past, unnecessary now that Canada has labour laws and minimum wages. Corporations have capitalized on this sentiment, suggesting that unionized workplaces are inefficient and outdated, and that unions just get in the way of healthy, fluid relationships between workers and management.

Just as discouraging, the Conservative government is now encroaching on workers' hard-won right to strike. In June 2011, the Harper government enacted back-to-work legislation after postal workers went on a rotating strike and were subsequently locked out of work by Canada Post. The Canadian Postal Workers Union is challenging the legality of this legislation. In March 2012, similar legislation was used to prevent Air Canada workers from striking. Without the right to strike—or even to present a legitimate threat of strike action—unions lose one of their key bargaining chips.

"The influence of unions has slowly been diminishing," says Andy Neufeld, director of communications and education at United Food and Commercial Workers Local 1518, which, along with UFCW local 247, represents most of the unionized supermarket workers in B.C. (As the largest retail union in Canada, UFCW would have been the most likely union for Dunlop and his coworkers to join.) Flagging awareness is exacerbated in the retail sector by the huge number of young workers with no previous union experience, he says. About sixty-five percent of workers in his local are under the age of thirty. Many have little or no previous experience with unions.

Neufeld makes an extra effort to capture the enthusiasm of these workers, many of whom are disinclined to pay union dues and don't see the benefit of membership—proven wage premiums, increased job security, better benefits, and a chance to have a stronger voice in the workplace. Neufeld says the union is trying to get this message out there, but is sending information into a glutted market. "We're competing for people's attention," he adds, "just like everybody else."

Young workers also have a high turnover rate (the turnover rate in Canada's retail sector is twenty-five percent), making it difficult to keep a strong, stable core of workers in place long enough to push an organizing drive through to success. Dunlop has firsthand experience with this phenomenon: During the course of his rabble rousing, half a dozen potential allies quit or were fired. Neufeld says high turnover is the number one cause for stagnating unionization rates in retail. It's no happy accident, either. "Employers can rely on this churn in the base of the workforce," Neufeld says.

In fact, at Whole Foods many of those interested in the idea of collective bargaining were afraid of reprisal to the point of inaction. Even Dunlop worried his union talk would find its way to management before he was ready—lest he prematurely land in hot water. As Dunlop puts it: "Nobody likes to stick their neck out."

Kyle Attwaters and Jillian Brooks were fellow meat clerks at the Whole Foods in Vancouver. (Brooks was employed from April 2009 to October 2009; Attwaters from January 2010 to May 2010.) Both are in their mid-twenties and both say they would have signed union cards despite their fear of being fired at a time when unemployment was high. When asked how they perceived the store's attitude toward unions, their responses are unqualified. "It was very frowned upon," Attwaters says. "They told us that right off the bat." Brooks is more frank: "The mention of unionizing would piss so many people off."

Attwaters says that when he first started at Whole Foods, he had to watch an introductory video with a segment on unions. He says that although the video didn't expressly forbid workers from unionizing or engaging in organizing activity, the message was clear that workers didn't need a union—Whole Foods' employment system worked fine without one. That system, it turns out, is to dictate the terms of employment and working conditions, leaving workers to accept them or find another job. Neufeld explains that employers are able to exploit their daily interaction with workers to influence opinion: "They're able to convince employees that they're better off without unions," he says. "Employees are very quick to pick up on those cues."

Whole Foods CEO John Mackey has been infamously outspoken in his contempt for unions. He once told a reporter in the '80s: "The union is like having herpes. It doesn't kill you, but it's unpleasant and inconvenient and stops a lot of people from becoming your lover." This strong anti-union sentiment is woven into the ethos of his 300-plus stores. (As of press time, Whole Foods had seven stores across British Columbia and Ontario, six in the UK, with the rest in the States.) Like many corporate retail stores, Whole Foods carries its fight against unions—and its own boosterism for the company—right down to the language workers are required to use. Whole Foods doesn't have employees or workers or clerks; it has "team members." And, despite clear distinctions in authority, there are no bosses or managers, only "team leaders."

In December, for instance, Dunlop submitted a long list of grievances to store team leaders. Among his complaints was unpaid overtime. At closing time, he'd observed workers clocking out and then returning to finish tidying up the area, readying it for the next day. Dunlop participated in this process once, on his first day. But when he realized nobody was getting paid for this extra work, he raised the matter with his superiors. Dunlop says that in the resulting conference between himself and an assistant store team leader, the team leader insisted on stressing the distinction in terminology—namely, Dunlop's use of the word manager— before addressing any of his actual complaints.

Such workplace jargon exists to influence the way employees perceive their relationship to the store—and it works. The idea is to create a feeling of allegiance to the company and not to fellow workers. "It was extremely difficult to convince people that workers and management have mutually antagonistic interests," says Dunlop.

In a list of things to expect during an organizing drive, the UFCW cites the "We're a family, we're a team" line as a likely scare tactic employed by companies. In some cases, as at Whole Foods, this team approach is undertaken pre-emptively to stop workers from even considering an organizing initiative, as it might be seen

85

as playing for the other side. But capitalism by nature pits labour and management against each other. Management is interested in minimizing costs, which means keeping wages low; labour is interested in maximizing wages. These fundamental differences in interest make it impossible to be part of the same team.

Once obtained, union certification is a challenge to maintain. Wal-Mart shut down its Jonquière, Quebec store in 2005 six months after workers voted to unionize (and failed to reach a collective agreement). More recently, in 2011, Target expanded into Canada, buying out over a hundred Zellers stores, including a handful of unionized locations. It refuses to honour any union contracts and is planning to fire all current Zellers employees. Instead, Target welcomes employees to reapply for non-union positions, foregoing any accumulated wage increases or benefits they may have earned over years of work. The biggest push to unionize a Whole Foods store was in Madison, Wisconsin in the early 2000s. Although workers voted for union certification, contract negotiations were drawn out for years and the union effort eventually ran out of worker support—especially after Mackey showed up at the store to hand out pamphlets titled "Beyond Unions." When Madison decertified in 2004, Mackey went on a nine-month "Beyond Unions" tour of his stores.

If unions are to stay relevant, they have to adapt. In some ways, they seem to be trying. The UFCW now requires every one of its locals to devote ten percent of resources to organizing initiatives, leading to some positive results. Earlier this year, a Future Shop in Montreal gained union certification. And in late 2011, an H&M store in Mississauga became the first in Canada to unionize, prompting organizing activities in many other locations. Notably, the campaign used social media to keep young workers interested in the drive. The UFCW has also launched a campaign to fight the anti-union Target takeover of Zellers. The "Target for Fairness" campaign raises awareness of Target's plans for Zellers workers and awareness billboards have been erected in cities across the country.

More innovation is still key. Unions need to be more creative in their organizing approaches, says University of Manitoba labour studies professor David Camfield. One of the best ways for unions to increase appeal, he adds, is to engage in significant action—something they've been doing less and less. This may mean more strike action, more political action, or even stronger responses to concession demands by employers. "It's not a question of sticking with the tried and true," Camfield says. "There's a lot of room for experimentation."

Part of this experimentation has to include greater democracy within unions, allowing for an increase in both worker participation and worker control. Enduring change must come from the bottom up. Currently, most unions are controlled by a small number of officials, who dictate how the organization will run. "Unions need to become more worker-driven, worker-run," says Camfield, "and that will only happen when workers themselves make it happen."

Unfortunately, current economic conditions aren't exactly encouraging workers to engage in union activity. Camfield says that higher unemployment and low job security have contributed to an environment in which workers are encouraged to compete amongst themselves. Such a situation is disastrous for the idea of solidarity, but it's terrific for employers, who constantly promote it, even with initiatives as seemingly harmless as Employee of the

Month awards. In the difficulties and discouragements, though, Camfield also sees opportunities for workers to find commonalities with each other, to identify and work with each other rather than submit to competition. "There are all sorts of ways," he says, "in which people could see that collective action would be a much better way to solve our problems than by being pitted against each other."

Recent activism have proven the power of solidarity and collective action. The Occupy movement, the Arab Spring, the student protests in Quebec have all brought huge masses of people together to resonating effect. Camfield says that these examples of effective collective action outside of the workplace can serve as inspiration; they could have the potential to feed into the workplace by influencing the way workers think about what they can achieve and how they can achieve it.

Had Dunlop stayed at Whole Foods longer, he might have been able to do more—of course, that's largely the point. Dunlop was fired after six months. He says he arrived to work one day in April, was allowed to work for one hour, then told to go home. He adds a store manager alleged he'd uttered a threat of physical harm against his immediate supervisor, a claim Dunlop disputes. Whole Foods has faced previous allegations of firing pro-union employees on trumped-up charges. During the campaign in Madison, two of the workers involved in the organizing activity were reportedly fired for dubious reasons. One of them made a latte the wrong way and gave this defective beverage to her co-worker instead of throwing it out. Both were let go for their parts in this breach of store policy.

Dunlop filed a claim with the labour board in November 2010 for having been fired without cause or notice. He says although Whole Foods maintained that they had sufficient grounds for dismissal, they decided to settle the matter without litigation. Dunlop was paid the week's worth of wages to which workers are entitled when fired without notice. He is now using his knowledge of labour law to help former coworkers challenge the power of the corporation. He has written a letter to the store managers offering his experience free of charge to anyone who's been fired from Whole Foods. It's a small, but cheeky contribution that helps him feel like he and his fellow workers haven't been pushed to resignation.

As Dunlop sits in his kitchen, finishing his budget salami sandwich, he says he's not surprised by his lack of success—he feels the deck was stacked against him. He doesn't regret the effort, though. "We have to try to stand together," he says. "If we don't at least try, where are we?"

Building Cities, Making Friends:
A Meditation, in Five General Propositions
Mark Kingwell

> *Like a bad concert hall, affective space contains dead spots where the sound fails to circulate.—The perfect interlocutor, the friend, is he not the one who constructs around you the greatest possible resonance? Cannot friendship be defined as a space with total sonority?*
>   —Roland Barthes, *A Lover's Discourse: Fragments*[1]

I am much taken with this image from Barthes' poignant, fragmentary, nuanced engagement with the plight of the lover, stranded at the limits of language. All love is a kind of wish, and here we see the core of all human longing, the desire for someone who will listen. There is no better figure of friendship than the implied construction of the good concert hall, the one where there are no dead spots, where I am always heard because you, the friend, have created a space so sonorous that my merest whisper is heard in the rear balcony.

Friendship, especially of the intimate sort that Barthes has in mind for the lover, may seem an odd keynote for a discussion of urbanism and architecture. But I want to suggest that the prospect of such intimacy, the space of total sonority, is the regulative ideal of all great cities, the goal, perhaps finally unreachable, towards which all effort is aimed. The construction of a resonance that allows each one of us to know that we are heard, that we have a friend in the existence of the city itself.

The image reverberates in another, more obvious way in the current context, of course, because the impressively varied practice of KPMB now includes one of the most perfectly sonorous concert halls to be found anywhere in Toronto, the city where I live, Koerner Hall, part of the Royal Conservatory of Music renovation of 2009. I was able to visit the site of this construction before it was completed, and climbed the scaffolded height to stand inside what would eventually become the elaborate wave-wood ceiling of this exemplary space. That is, I was able to stand inside one of the design elements that make for sonority in the finished hall. That moment of suspension within a not-yet-finished architectural project remains, for me, a crystallized memory of what it means to build a city, to create the material conditions of shared dwelling. And now, when I step into the hall's lobby, which floats over Philosopher's Walk, the park-like thorough fare that connects Bloor Street with the nearby university, and embraces downtown Toronto as if we were in a living room—or a shared playground—I see again the genius of this design.

The meditative origins, the warm materials palette, the creation of a community space and not just a building: these traits are characteristic of the KPMB practice. More than any other firm, KPMB has sounded the keynote of urban renewal in Toronto, their home base. But projects in other cities and towns are equally significant makers of sonority. If we believe Aristotle, that a just city must be, in some sense, a city of friends, the architectural interventions of KPMB are more than commissions or projects; they are exercises in civic humanism. Buildings become, in effect, miniature cities, gathering their surrounding spaces, large and small, unto themselves. From the modified college cloister of the CIGI Campus in Waterloo, Ontario (2011), with its stunning cantilevered entrance and warm interior spaces for conversation and instruction (which converts the loose edge of a small town into a vibrant urban site) to the capacious Vaughan City Hall (2011), Canada's National Ballet School (2005), the renovated Gardiner Museum (2006), and the TIFF Bell Lightbox (2011), we observe again and again the *material conditions of community.*

By that phrase I mean at least the following five necessary features of city building: (1) a strong connection to existing urban geography—even if, as in the Vaughan project, for example, the surrounding area is anti-aesthetic or bare; (2) the artful reinterpretation of traditional elements and forms (the courtyard, the quad, the bell tower, the café); (3) the creation of public space within buildings as well as between them, forming interior crucibles of shared citizenship; (4) programme design that makes for frequent mixing and social interplay; and, perhaps above all, (5) a sense of *play*, the ability to create spontaneous situations and encounters among people, to achieve even in workmanlike spaces a creative, non-utilitarian *dérive*—a drift.[2]

Since these five features may seem obvious, even as their realization is in fact far from common, allow me to expand on them with a series of expansive theses which I believe the city-building practice of KPMB brings to our attention. Thus a meditation, philosophical and architectural, in the form of five general propositions ...

GENERAL PROPOSITION NO. 1:
The city is a philosophical extension of the human person.

This proposition is valid along at least two distinct vectors. First, the city is an extension of human action in the same way that Marshall McLuhan meant when he said that communications media are 'extensions of man.' Media enables a routine transcendence of the limitations which inhere in the human sensorium. Unaided, I can see only what is revealed to my eyes, hear only what lies within range of my ears, and so on. But with the aid of a telephone, or a television, or a telegrap—with, to be sure, a computer or tablet but also, for that matter, with smoke signals or a walking stick cane—I can experience a vastly expanded range of possible stimuli beyond my meagre bodily range: events, stories, intimacies. Media offers us an extended body, a body stretched and attenuated across large distances in space and time.

The built environment of the city is, by the same logic, a massive and complex extension of the human body. It allows me precisely to pursue all the bodily tasks of human life that make for the complex achievement of personhood: to shelter and work, to move and interact, to eat and drink, to remember and forget, to live, love and die. Not all of its extensions are strictly sensory, as in communications media as such; instead, the city is what we might call the ur-medium or super-extension of man. The city offers ways of getting somewhere, places worth getting to, places that are neither here nor there. The person, in the form of his or her body, perforce negotiates these spaces on a daily basis—and so comes into contact with other persons, other bodies, doing the same. The city is thus the physical manifestation of our desires and purposes, both responsive to what we think we want and constraining, shaping, of what we come to want.

It has been a commonplace at least since Aristotle (him again!) that first we create cities, and then they create us. Winston Churchill's much-quoted line to the same effect, where the term 'buildings' appears in the place of 'cities,' is both less general and offered without proper provenance. He is not wrong, but the deeper point—the point that lurks in Aristotle's sense of the city as an expression of organic norms encoded in the natural *and* social world (really there is no bright division between them)—is that buildings affect other buildings as well as affecting people. Cities are composed of complexes of desire, not all of which are entirely conscious at the level of the individual user or even creator of buildings.[3]

The general proposition is valid in another, perhaps less obvious sense, however. It is related to the first but requires a little more philosophical flexibility to accept. It is this: the city is, like the human person, subject to a version of the mind-body problem. That problem, with us since Descartes, concerns that apparently mysterious causal linkage between one substance, the mind, which is wholly immaterial, with another, the body, which is wholly non-mental. (The Homer Simpson version goes like this: 'Mind? No matter. Matter? Never mind.') How is it possible that the human person, apparently possessed, somehow, of both a distinct mind and an ambulatory body, is able to function? On the premise of two distinct substances, this should not be possible; and yet, the evidence is overwhelmingly in favour of its being not only possible, but trivial. People do things each and every day, blithely unaware that there is any problem at all concerning the interaction of the mental and the material.

We need not tarry here with Descartes' proposed solution to the problem (a neatly evasive reference to a mysterious substance-interface performed in the pineal gland) nor with the many decades, indeed centuries, of debate that this problem has spawned. What we can do, instead, is note that there is a rather obvious solution to the mind-body problem, which is in fact dissolution: the premise of two wholly distinct substances is flawed from the start. Human consciousness is not, despite philosophers' longstanding penchant for abstraction and out-of-body thought experiments, ever divorced from its embodiment; by the same token, the human body is not best conceived as some inanimate machine which receives a jolt of life from the ghostly inhabitation of mental activity. This point can be made as a matter of logic, as Gilbert Ryle did: his dismissive phrase 'the ghost in the machine' for the Cartesian orthodoxy is deployed in my previous sentence.[4] It can also be made positively, via the introduction of an alternative view.

There are several such alternatives, but the most persuasive is some version of what has come to be called phenomenology. On this view, it is impossible to conceive of human consciousness without an awareness of the facts of embodiment. Consciousness just is a sense of being somewhere, in place, that complex immersion of self within a horizon of spatial and temporal awareness. To be myself (to be anyone at all) is to presuppose, as a condition of life's possibility, a sense of *in front* and *behind*, *here* and *there*, *then* and *now*. That premise—and not some division of substances manufactured in the laboratory of runaway meditation—is the philosophically significant fact about human persons. And it is realized in a host of daily actions and experiences, from the skillful but mostly implicit negotiation of myself through a doorway—together with the loss of memory that such a threshold-crossing may entail!—to the complex bobbing and weaving required to traverse a busy sidewalk or railway-station concourse.[5]

We may seem to have wandered some distance from cities, and architecture, and architects. But not really. For a city entertains and then solves—or rather, dissolves—its own version of the mind-body problem in just the same way. A city is not reducible just to its built forms: on the analogy, its matter or 'body.' But neither is the city merely the sum total of its citizens and their desires: again, per analogy, its consciousness or 'mind.' And just as neither of these reductions can be validly enacted, since each limits the reality of the city as a living thing, an achievement, it is likewise the case that the city is not best conceived as some troubled interaction between the two aspects. Indeed, the sense of division between built forms and citizen-desires is precisely the premise that requires dismissal. Phenomenology sees the human person as embodied consciousness; good urban theory views the city the same way.[6]

GENERAL PROPOSITION NO. 2:

The architect is an instinctive phenomenologist of the city.

Architecture concerns the unfinished text of the city: the city is never over, always begun anew, ever layered. Architecture creates public space even when its projects are nominally private—an office building rather than a park or institution—because the architect's intervention is made within the shared fabric of the city. That noun 'fabric,' so often used without full awareness, creates a trace of meaning worth following, a thread to tease out: a fabric is not just textile but, instead, any made thing, that which is fabricated. The shared urban fabric is the making, the project, which engages and concerns us all. The city, the made thing which we inhabit, is our collective project. But the architect has a special status within this shared fabrication.

That master of the paradoxical thought, Pascal, said this about our status as *thinking reeds*—"the most feeble thing in nature,"—but blessed with the significant, indeed transcendent ability to consider ourselves: "It is not from space that I must seek my dignity, but from the government of my thought. I shall have no more if I possess worlds. By space, the universe envelops me and swallows me up like a point; by thought, I envelop the world."[7] Here consciousness flies out and back in an instant, and the occupation of space is revealed for what it is: a speculation by consciousness about consciousness, a thought about the very fact of thinking. This moment of reflection—which is the moment in which consciousness experiences itself *as self*—is architecture's business and highest achievement.

But (one might object) surely architecture is about solving technical issues in the deployment of space, heating and cooling, and programme, the negotiation of site and client desire? Of course it is. But to what purpose? If architecture is not a form of speculation about life, the occasion for thought, it has failed its ultimate mission. That is why, contrary to the usual narratives of ego and mannerism, the real objections to signature style or grand formalist gestures in an architect are not about humility but, instead, concern rigour of thought. The architect who indulges style over conversation—with the adjacent buildings and streets, with the citizens, with the city—has failed to engage the philosophical responsibilities of the architect. He or she may have failed other responsibilities as well: aesthetic, political, ethical; but these are predicated on the more basic failure to *think*.

One therefore looks at this urban thought in action—in Concordia University's integrated complex combining faculties for

Engineering, Computer Science, Visual Arts and Business (2005 and 2009), for example, with its deft vertical integration of an otherwise inchoate campus stranded in a downtown neighbourhood in Montréal that has heretofore lacked a coherent identity—and feels a power of thoughtful consideration, the way design is executed at the service of community and use. Other campus projects—for Centennial and George Brown colleges (2004 and 2012), future works at M.I.T., Princeton and Northwestern universities—demonstrate the same sensitivity to gathering and listening. Indeed, we might say that here campus and city become specular partners: the urban college or university folded into the city surround, but also the isolated campus made into a miniature city.

Campus in Latin means field, and the first university campuses were not the quads and towers but the fields on which they sat; now, a campus is a field of thought, a field of possibility, at once delineated and opened by the built forms in which we work, speculate and converse. Discourse, realized in matter, enabling discourse.

GENERAL PROPOSITION NO. 3:
Not all great architecture is great urban architecture.

The reason for this distinction should be obvious. There are great architects and (it follows) great buildings which do not concern themselves with city building. Such buildings may inhabit cities, or stand in their precincts, but they do not engage and converse with the city. Hence these are buildings that do not build the city—they are not part of its shared fabric. It is possible for such buildings to be monuments, in Aldo Rossi's sense, but only in the somewhat violent sense that they take up and redistribute the existing surround without regard for its history of effects. We might, indeed, distinguish here between violent monuments and benign ones, the latter embodying more of Rossi's sense that a city could be memorialized and extended by the monumental in architecture.[8]

Thus, one might include in the former, violent category such examples as the Eiffel Tower in Paris and Daniel Libeskind's Michael Lee-Chin Crystal renovation of the Royal Ontario Museum in Toronto, and in the latter category the Empire State Building in Manhattan and, in Toronto, the John P. Robarts Research Library at the University of Toronto. Note that the distinction is not a function of modest elevation or of accommodating style: the Empire State soars but nevertheless manages to engage and (we might say) *shelter* its island home; the concrete brutalist mass of Robarts is surprisingly warm, even welcoming. The affectionate nickname it has earned from students at the University of Toronto—Fort Book—communicates benign monumentality better than any amount of theoretical discourse.[9]

The conclusion I mean to derive from these rather tendentious examples (for what examples are not tendentious when we speak of architecture and theory?) is that sometimes, maybe often, the 'bold' or 'original' architectural statement is precisely the one that does not succeed in building the city. There is surely a place for signature buildings and insistent gestural design in all great cities—one might even argue that no city can be truly great without the spirited conversation, or controversy, that inevitably erupts around such buildings. But they do not, themselves, make the city; in fact, they are parasitic upon another kind of architectural genius, namely the sort that intervenes in and subtly extends existing conversations, not splashing but rippling the waters of urban life.

Pedestrians may not stop on the street to take photographs of such buildings, but one must concede at a certain point that this is the point. A photographed building may be a mere oddity, a sport, a folly. More nuanced regard may be present in the form of quiet approval, pleasant engagement, calm beauty. This is the stillness of perfect form, which yet works a sly magic on the viewer and user, stretching the boundaries of consciousness in ways more powerful for being less jarring.

GENERAL PROPOSITION NO. 4:
Urban architecture is, above all, the creation of place.

There is a line from David Young's play Inexpressible Island, about the bare survival of a Royal Navy expedition to Antarctica, which has stayed with me since I saw the original production in 1997. In the drama, based on historical events, six men are lost in the extreme landscape near the South Pole at the same time that Robert Scott's ill-fated Terra Nova expedition is perishing of cold and starvation. The six figures in the play will all survive, barely, the brutal eight months of winter, only to find their story overshadowed by the harrowing tale of Scott's failure. The play is about many things, including class and spirituality, but mostly it shows the weirdly inspired madness that can descend on human beings undergoing desperate conditions of life. Towards the end of the winter, the small unit's medical officer, Dr. Levick, descends into a kind of philosophical delirium.

"Nature, in the form of man, begins to recognize itself," Levick says, ostensible to his command officer, Lieutenant Campbell, but really to himself. "That's what we're doing here in the South, Lieutenant. We are all artists, of a kind. We are giving nature back to herself." And, later: "As much as anything that's what has carried us here on this pilgrimage. The South Pole is an idea. A place that is no place. The final nothing."[10]

There is much to consider in these lines, as in the whole play. The South Pole is an abstraction, a notional point created only by the world-defining Cartesian geometry of the Mercator Projection. It is both real and not real: a place that is not a place, something that does not exist for humans yet can be fixed, and visited for the first time (as we know, it would be Scott's tragedy to find that Norwegian rival Roald Amundsen had beaten him to the spot). Thus this is a pilgrimage of the mind, carried out by the body. A modern spiritual journey, a *hejira* defined entirely by lines, angles and national identity. But it is also a work of art: the creation of that place where the mind and the body meet— perhaps to perish—where the universe becomes aware of itself in the form of human consciousness. Nature, in the form of man, begins to recognize itself.

All creation of place exhibits this eerie mixture of abstract and concrete, of material and mental. And so we return again to the basic phenomenological awareness of embodied consciousness, but now tied even more closely to the idea of place, of being in place by deploying the conditions of possibility for place-making. Anywhere—and, it follows, nowhere—can be a place. As long as we are there, to think and talk, to listen and respond. The world, once conscious of itself in the form of human making, is a vast concert hall. What sounds there is not the divine music of celestial spheres, as the ancient Greek mathematicians believed, but the sound of one human after another issuing the daily plea: to be heard, to be understood, to be accommodated.

And, invoking another play about survival, extremity and madness, we know that the opposite condition, the poor, bare, forked condition of human alienation, is precisely the lack of place: the heath, where Lear must go mad because he is not, finally, heard. Reason not the need!

GENERAL PROPOSITION NO. 5:
The creation of place is the gift of play.

A gift is given without expectation of return. In the true gift economy, wealth is measured not by how much one has accumulated but by how much one has given away. Truly to give, to give beyond all exchange or reciprocity, is to be irresponsible, creative, ironic, spontaneous, available. It is to play, in the sense that great art and great philosophy are forms of play.

Place-making is play-making. In one sense, to make a place is to create the material conditions of experience, to create the phenomenological clearing; but a place is not a place without my being there, my finding myself there, being in place. Further, place-making does not end with the subjective experience of either the one-in-place or the maker-of-place. For it is the nature of places to keep on giving, to create and renew, again and again, the conditions of their own possibility. Places are, in a sense, living things, maintained in time by experience and enjoyment. That is what it is for a place to be a place. This is what it means to clear a space for us to play in.

City halls, educational buildings, cinematic complexes—functionality varies according to task. Place-making, and hence city-building, transcends all specific functionality. It speaks to engagement, not programme, freedom rather than function.

It is in such places that we may find—or (as we sometimes say) *make*—friends. There may be in actuality no perfect interlocutor as described by Barthes, but the well-built city gives us the chance, over and over, to try and find that comprehensively resonant friend. The one with whom we can play. The one who will listen while we drift together, continuously.

END NOTES

[1] Roland Barthes, *A Lover's Discourse: Fragments* (Paris, Éditions du Seuil, 1977; Hill & Wang, Richard Howard, trans., 1978, 2010), p. 167, from the fragment 'No Answer: mutisme/silence.'

[2] Though I borrow here the term favoured by the Situationists, there is no need to align the sort of city-building I am discussing, with its feet firmly rooted in reality, alongside the utopian New Babylon 'city of play' advocated by Ivan Chtcheglov and Constant Nieuwenhuys. Still, there is something compelling about the vision of a city designed entirely for *homo ludens*, a city where, as Chtcheglov puts it in his 'Formulary for a New Urbanism,' ' [t]he main activity of the inhabitants will be CONTINUOUS DRIFTING.' Chtcheglov promises an 'aesthetic of behaviours' but also a 'complete phenomenology of couples, encounters, and duration.' Along the way, he reserves some choice words for Le Corbusier: 'Some sort of psychological repression dominates this individual—whose face is as ugly as his conception of the world—such that he wants to squash people under ignoble masses of reinforced concrete, a noble material that should rather be used to enable an aerial articulation of space that could surpass the flamboyant Gothic style. His cretinizing influence is immense. A Le Corbusier model is

the only image that arouses in me the idea of immediate suicide. He is destroying the last remnants of joy. And of love, passion, freedom.' (See http://www.bopsecrets.org/SI/Chtcheglov.htm.) Chtcheglov first drafted the 'Formulary' in 1953, when he was 19, under the name Gilles Ivain; it was published in the first issue of *Internationale Situationniste*. He spent five years in a psychiatric ward after being committed by his wife, and died in 1998.

[3] A somewhat hostile review of my book *Nearest Thing to Heaven: The Empire State Building and American Dreams* (New Haven, Yale University Press, 2006) suggested that the claim there—namely, that the Empire State had in a sense 'caused' the people of New York to construct it, given the logic of the 'race for the sky,' contemporary technological advances, and so on—was evidence of my having been 'bamboozled' by fashionable French theory. No, just taking Aristotle seriously.

[4] See Gilbert Ryle, *The Concept of Mind* (New York, Hutchinson & Co., 1949).

[5] The congruence between phenomenological theory and clinical psychological findings is a growth industry in academia. Just one example: a 2011 University of Notre Dame study found that doors and other spatial thresholds created 'event boundaries' in episodes of experience or activity, prompting changes of consciousness that might, for example, present as changes of mood or, notoriously, temporary loss of memory. Hence the common experience, even absent dementia, of arriving in a room and not knowing what brought you there, or what you came to fetch. One of the study's authors offered this advice: 'Doorways are bad. Avoid them at all costs.' (Misty Harris, 'Study shows doors can be linked to memory loss,' *The National Post* [November 9, 2011]).

[6] This is an extremely brief rehearsal of arguments that I make at length in *Concrete Reveries: Consciousness and the City* (New York, Viking Adult, 2008).

[7] Pascal, *Pensées*, #348.

[8] Aldo Rossi, *Architecture of the City* (Cambridge, Mass., MIT Press, 1982). It is worth noting that Rossi considers himself, after a fashion, a structuralist devotee of Barthes.

[9] But for more theoretical discussion, see Mark Kingwell, 'Monumental-Conceptual Architecture,' *Harvard Design Magazine* 19 (Fall 2003/Winter 2004) and also *Nearest Thing to Heaven*, ed. cit., passim.

[10] David Young, *Inexpressible Island* (Winnipeg, Scirocco Drama, 1998), pp. 116 and 120.

The Murders in the Mine
Katherine Laidlaw

On May 22, 1992, a company called Royal Oak Mines Inc. locked out its workforce at Giant Mine in Yellowknife. The union, the local 4 chapter of the Canadian Association of Smelter and Allied Workers, and management couldn't reach a settlement. Before the strike, it was a good, if finite, time to be a gold miner. The average worker at Giant was pulling in $77,000 a year, and those clocking overtime were making more than $100,000. But the strike got dirty quickly as rumours swirled of Royal Oak CEO Peggy Witte's intent to break the union. One thing she did break was an unwritten labour rule in Canada: you don't bring in replacement workers. No mining company had done that in forty-five years. Nevada-born Witte flew them in by helicopter the next day.

From there, things got scary. Profane strike posters littered the route along the highway to the mine. An underwear-clad Miss Piggy doll was mounted on a stake, her neck circled by a noose, head dangling and blond curls blowing in the wind. Both sides hurled vulgarities across the gate at the mine entrance. In June, a riot broke out, as RCMP and Pinkerton guards—hired to act as the mine's security force—clashed with strikers who tore down the mine fence and swarmed the grounds. Nearly thirty people were charged. Two months later, a group of strikers calling themselves the Cambodian Cowboys began to break into the mine, spray-painting anti-scab graffiti on its underground walls, blowing up a satellite dish on the townsite and later using explosives to shut down one of the mine's ventilation shafts.

And then the bomb went off, killing nine men—six line-crossers and three replacement workers—and setting in motion a 13-month-long criminal investigation and fifteen years of criminal trials and civil lawsuits. If you lived in Yellowknife in September 1992, you remember where you were when the blast went off. You remember that girl at school saying loudly that she had biked out to the site and witnessed the carnage with her own eyes. You remember the worried creases in your mom's face as she dialed the same number over and over, trying to get your dad on the line. You remember your classmate's desk sitting empty that day, knowing he lived out at Giant, being afraid for him. You remember your dad warning you not to go out that night, to stay home and stay safe. If you were one of the 15,000 people who spent that year watching Yellowknife descend into violent, rabid madness, it's a time you don't forget.

Leslie Creed is a Giant Mine baby. For as long as she can remember, her dad worked at the mine. Her folks moved there the year after she was born, 1981, and stayed until the mine closed eighteen years later. The Creed family lived in one of the many identical brown duplexes that overlooked the busiest boat launch in town, down the road from the headframe on the shores of Great Slave Lake. Families came and went every few years—moving into their own places in town or leaving Yellowknife entirely. But the Creeds stayed: Leslie's dad working in the refinery laying gold bricks; her mom sunbathing nude with the other miners' wives, hidden from the view of the highway. Leslie and her brother and sister were part of the Giant pack, growing up on the rocks outside of town. It was idyllic.

"We ran wild. We'd have fires on the rocks. We would use the pipeboxes as our pathways into the mine site," she says. "It was a community. We always had Christmas parties together. We would all trudge as a little group of kids for Hallowe'en, going from house to house to house, trick-or-treating."

Her first twelve years were blessed with a carefree spirit, like growing up camping, but with electricity, she says. Then, in 1992, the miners went on strike. First, changes came slowly. A picket line was erected at the townsite entrance. After a while, the Giant dwellers weren't allowed to use the townsite gates anymore, and had to go through the mine itself. The Pinkerton guards came to live on the site for a while, to keep an eye out. Then, things got more serious. The school bus the Giant kids took to school every day was blocked at the gates by the strikers. "They stopped the bus and they said, 'we're getting on,'" Creed says. They walked the aisles, searching the bus for replacement workers or family members coming in and out. The satellite dish next to the Creeds' house was blown up. Kids at school were bullied or shunned. "It was really weird going to school and seeing kids wear 'no scab' buttons on their clothes, in elementary school, junior high. I couldn't believe that their parents would encourage them to wear those things," she says. "I remember my teachers asking us how we were doing out there."

The morning of September 18, Leslie was home from school. She was sick with a cold and was waiting for her dad, who was in management at the mine, to drive her into town to the doctor. She felt the vibrations shake the townsite. Just another blast, she thought. The tremors through the kitchen floor were nothing new. But her dad was extra-quiet that morning. And as they wound their way out to the mine entrance, Leslie realized something was seriously wrong. "It was an absolutely crazy amount of people. Military, RCMP, strikers, families, news reporters. That's when my dad told me what happened. There was an explosion, he said. Some people were killed."

When she got home from the doctor, her parents began packing up her things. They sent Leslie and her siblings to live with family friends in town for three weeks. "I hated being away from home. But at that point, you didn't know what they were capable of anymore. They blew up our satellite dish, next to my house. They blew up a trolley car with men in it. What's next?" That year, none of the Giant kids were allowed to trick-or-treat.

For Jamesie Fournier, it's the slight flicking sound of playing cards he recalls when he thinks about the strike. It was late at night, when his mom and dad would sit religiously playing cards, that he'd hear about the ugliness at the mine. He was eight, son to wild-haired miner Jim Fournier, also known as Rags. At first, before things got too violent, he and his little brother had spent a lot of time on the line, eating egg-salad sandwiches, sipping ginger ale and feeling like pirates standing on top of a shelled-out school bus brandishing binoculars and keeping a stern eye on things. "You felt like you were on an outpost in the middle of nowhere," he says.

To the young Fournier the battle lines seemed clear—a feisty union versus greedy management, a man's means versus his principles. He was proud of his dad. He was fighting the oppressors! He was standing up for his community! "It was a really fun time. We enjoyed it," he says now, a slight, dark-haired 28-year-old with thick black earrings in his ears. But, one day in June, the boys weren't allowed to go. "I remember the day we were supposed to go. We were all ready and my dad came home at the last minute and said, 'I don't think you boys should be coming today.'" The boys argued, the protest signs they'd made lying dejectedly on the floor, but their father in his ragged union cap wouldn't budge. He knew it wouldn't be safe—tempers were flaring and that day there'd be a fight.

Later that night, Fournier listened from his bedroom to the cards smacking the table as his dad told his mom about the riot-police clubbing their shields that day, about strikers throwing rocks, tear-gas streaming and attack dogs growling. His dad had run onto the mine grounds with the others, dodging gunfire as an officer popped off warning shots. He stopped when he saw a guard collapse in a pond on the site. Picking up a rock, he heaved it into the air, poised to bring it down on the guard lying in the muck. He slammed it to the ground, missing the guard's head. The flicking of the cards stopped after that, for the three months his dad went to jail.

As money got tight, luxuries gradually went away. My dad told me, "Things are going to be changing now James. We're going to go from one of Yellowknife's highest paid [families] to not paid at all." Fournier remembers being given super-soaker waterguns by his friend's dad because his parents couldn't buy them. He remembers other families on their block giving his parents food when they cleared out their refrigerators before leaving on vacation. He remembers no-name macaroni-and-cheese, Cheez Whiz, no longer having cable TV. "When they used to have hot-dog days and pizza days in school, we'd never be able to get that, so we'd always get the pizza crusts from the other kids," he says. "I really like pizza crusts now."

And yet, Fournier's memories of growing up on the line are fond ones. His dad coached his sports teams, at least until he couldn't anymore because he had a criminal record. He got to watch the Toronto Blue Jays win the '92 World Series in the union hall with his brother and his dad, swiping Oreo cookies from the area that was restricted from kids.

After the strike ended, Fournier says, the town quieted. "Things went back to normal for a bit, but you knew it wasn't going to last. And when the mine started shutting down, you could feel worry that it was going to become a ghost town. And then shortly after that, diamonds were found." Collective amnesia set in, he says. "I think everyone was wanting to move on."

Dale Johnston was running, shoes scraping against the gravel pebbles lining Yellowknife's streets. It was a phone she was after. Her pounding feet were the only sound ringing through her ears over the noise of the men yelling. She was scared.

Usually, she thought she was pretty tough. The daughter of a former union president and a staunch union family, she'd been one of the protestors at the riot that June day, bringing down the fence and swarming the mine site. She'd seen riot cops and tear gas and hurled profanities. She was involved. But tonight felt different. People were dead now. Her dad's friend was dead; she'd heard it on the radio at home that day. Her dad had warned her not to go out that night, but she figured going to see a movie couldn't hurt. Then the brawl broke out. She recognized the union guy getting beaten outside the bar by a group of men, shouting accusations, unleashing their pent-up frustration. She heard the clattering of glass and went for the closest payphone she could remember, a couple of blocks away.

"Stay low," the man at the union hall told her when she called. "Just stay low. Don't be out and about." You didn't know who could be hiding around the corner, beer bottle in hand. Everyone was feeling like a fight that night.

Today, Johnston is thirty-five years old, the mother of three young boys. She moved away from Yellowknife and so did her dad, both living in Grand Prairie, Alberta. But no matter what, or where, or who, every time she sees a picket line, she stops, circles the block to the nearest doughnut shop and parks her car. She never passes strikers, she says, without stopping to buy them coffee. She's a union girl.

The Giant Mine murders have brought Katie O'Neil to a little trailer on a Vancouver Island reserve. There, the twenty-two-year-old, freshly home from two years in Australia, sits with her father, Jim, once a miner at Giant. He sits in a lazy-boy recliner and she sits in a desk chair, facing a computer screen, a journal open on her lap. They write. Katie's story is different than the others. She was just two when the bomb went off. A memory she can barely recall has engulfed her whole life.

She doesn't remember the day her dad came home, rendered unable to speak for hours from the shock after he was one of the first to reach the blast scene. He looked desperately for his best friend, Chris Neill, and the eight other miners, but all that remained of them was flesh and bone blown into the mine walls. Katie remembers things in snapshots. "Sometimes pictures will bring back a memory. I saw a picture a while ago of the graffiti on the front of my house," she says, referring to the word "SCAB" vandals painted across her garage when her dad crossed the picket line. "And I remember sitting on the ground with a paintbrush in my hand and Chris Neill painting the front of our house because he was sick of looking at the graffiti." Another time, she says, she remembered dumping her crayons all over the floor. "I didn't do it, the strikers did it!" she explained to her mom. "I thought the strikers were boogey-men." The strike, for Katie, had become mythical. She knew what "striker" and "scab" meant by the time she was three years old.

Ten years ago, Jim O'Neil moved to a First Nations reserve on Vancouver Island. He's an RV repairman now—he stopped mining underground after the explosion. He tried to go back to work but the thought of the man-car shards in the tunnel walls underground—there's only so much a man can take. He's spent the past twenty years trying to reason away what he saw that day after the blast. "It's been a very, very lonely battle," he says.

He left Yellowknife, seeking treatment for post-traumatic stress disorder in Edmonton. After five years of therapy and little improvement, he went to work on a cattle ranch in Sherwood Park, Alberta. He and Katie's mother got divorced. He put wads of money into doctors and treatments. He has exaggerated startle response—a PTSD symptom that causes his body to jerk and shake violently when triggered—something he'll live with for the rest of his life. He has nightmares when he hears the word "union."

He's still looking for answers, finding holes in the RCMP's evidence against Roger Warren, the man jailed for setting the bomb. He thinks Warren took the rap for something he didn't do alone. "I've always thought that other people certainly knew what was going on," he says.

Now that the lawsuits are complete, now that the RCMP have disposed of the evidence, Katie and Jim spend days and nights—sometimes from "dusk until dawn"—poring over journals from that time, writing them into a book. When they finish, they'd like the book to be published. Catharsis, he hopes. "If I could truly say, yes, I know what happened to my friend Chris Neill and the other eight guys in Giant Mine, maybe then I could do something else without the interference of PTSD," Jim says. "Somehow, someday, there will be closure. There's got to be some better closure than I have right now."

For now, father and daughter sit in their chairs, listening to the beating of the drums in the longhouse, and drift away.

Yellowknife is a resilient, transient town and twenty years is a long time. Still, the strike lingers, in the faded union graffiti downtown, the former strikers and police officers who ignore each other at the grocery store, the friendships damaged irreparably. Al Shearing, the prime suspect in the police's case for a long time, still lives in town, scavenging at the dump in his pickup and working construction. He spent two-and-half years in jail for sneaking into the mine, painting anti-scab graffiti and blowing up a ventilation shaft. "I felt justified. I think I should have done more," he told the CBC in a 2003 interview. "They tried for 13 months and couldn't prove anything." Helen Warren, Roger Warren's wife, still lives in Yellowknife too, working for the government. (In a strange twist, Warren and Shearing are now related—Shearing married Kathy Hrynczuk, Helen's sister, ten years after the bombing.) Warren himself is jailed in Mission, B.C., at Ferndale Institution, a minimum-security prison. He's eligible for parole in 2015.

Speaking about the strike while answering to charges in court, striker Tim Bettger, the police's second suspect in their investigation, said: "None of the rules of the world seemed to apply any longer. For what it's worth, I want to apologize to my family." In his case, at least, the ending of William Golding's classic novel Lord of the Flies comes to mind: The boys disperse, stunned and appalled by the mob mentality that drove them to brutal violence. Ten years ago, one of the murdered miners' sons, Joe Pandev, told the local paper: "I want people to remember what happened and to be embarrassed by it. The way people acted, it was just embarrassing for a community to turn on itself like that. And over what?"

Not long after the strike, Royal Oak went bankrupt and walked away from Giant, saddling taxpayers with a $500-million cleanup bill. Above ground, the site is a mix of rickety wooden structures and sci-fi steel spires that shoot up from the rock. Below ground, a quarter-million tons of deadly arsenic fester in vast chambers. The government says in another decade, by the 30th anniversary of the murders, remediation will be complete. The mine will be clean, at least on the surface. But the waste underground, they say, will have to be monitored "in perpetuity." Deep down, things won't go away.

EDITOR'S NOTE: More than ten strikers were approached to be interviewed for this story, including Roger Warren. All of them declined.

Against Domesticated Fiction, or The Need For Re-enchantment

Patricia Robertson

It's all a question of story. We are in trouble just now because we are in between stories.
 —Thomas Berry
What's dying is the ability of conventional stories to carry meaning, to bear the burden.
 —A writer friend, by email
The medium itself has been hijacked. The storyteller has no story to tell and doesn't even know where to begin the new one.
 —Diarmuid O'Murchu

I. THE WORSHIP OF SELF

I feel an increasing sense of desperation these days as a writer. Many of us, it seems, are either overwhelmed by the sheer scale of the problems—climate change, biodiversity loss, collapsing financial systems, broken democracies—or in a state of denial, sleepwalking further into the nightmare. Yet at the same time a century's worth of quantum physics has revealed an extraordinary, paradigm-shifting world, one that offers us a completely new, intimately interconnected model of the universe. In every sense of the word we live in extraordinary times, poised on a knife-edge between tremendous possibility and tremendous urgency.

Faced with all this, what are writers doing? Most of them, with a few honourable exceptions, seem barely to have noticed, judging by the fiction, poetry, and creative nonfiction being produced these days. Either they're pretending the postmodernist avant-garde experiment is still relevant or they're flogging the dead horse of modernism. "A society experiencing a genuine emergency, as we often claim to be, would see that reflected in its cultural output," says the British writer and environmental activist Paul Kingsnorth. "What we have instead is a *fin-de-siècle* culture. We subsist on a tedious diet of novels about inner-city kidz or country-house angst; poetry that examines the poets' inner life in arrhythmic stanzas; visual art playing games with empty cynicism, its creators swanning about like catwalk-models complaining about their tax-brackets. It's as if nothing were ever going to change; as if nothing were changing already."

In Canada, that *fin-de-siècle* culture, that frivolous entertainment and spectacle, takes the form of increasing numbers of literary prizes and galas, literary wrestling matches such as CBC's "Canada Reads," and writers' conferences where writers are briefly accorded the status of celebrities. We are adrift in sensationalism, marketability, the turning of authors into brand names—perfect commodities for the Age of Commodification. "Aesthetic narcissism," says the New Zealand poet Denys Trussell, "is inevitable in an age of social and ecological breakdown." In such an environment, the fact that good work is still, sometimes, written is little short of miraculous.

The Globe and Mail recently ran a series asking writers what it was like to be a writer in Canada. The responses were filled mostly with burbling approval. It took a writer born elsewhere, the Greek-Canadian playwright and novelist Pan Bouyoucas, to be more critical:

> Canadian writers, at least my generation of Canadian writers, are a
> privileged lot. We can write about anything we want without getting
> arrested for it or shot ... Why then—and here is maybe the downside
> of so much peace and freedom—do I often get the feeling of reading
> the same story, over and over? A story where nothing much happens,

empty of magic, filled with navel-gazing and gloom and piddling private conversations commenting every wart and fart to death.

The answer to Bouyoucas' question lies partly in the need to sensationalize the self, as described above, but also in the somnolence induced by late-stage fundamentalist capitalism. Many of us, in pursuing the modernist agenda to its conclusion (and beyond), have colluded with the capitalist agenda of the individual self, a self who is not (except in the most romanticized ways) part of a family, certainly not part of a community, and most definitely not a citizen with a role to play in the public sphere. We, like the books we produce, have become products. We have forfeited the right to speak on behalf of the soul by our collusion, our unwillingness to speak up. I think, with some shame, of the Russian poet Anna Akhmatova, describing her role as a poet during the Stalinist era:

> During the terrible years of the Yekhov terror I spent seventeen months in the prison queues in Leningrad. One day someone 'identified' me. Then a woman with lips blue with cold who was standing behind me, and of course had never heard of my name, came out of the numbness which affected us all and whispered in my ear—(we all spoke in whispers there): 'Could you describe this?' I said, 'I can!' Then something resembling a smile slipped over what had once been her face.

That devastating final phrase—"what had once been her face"—seems to me to apply to all of us under global capitalism. Of course one can argue that there have always been oppressive regimes reducing their citizens to facelessness. But now there are seven billion of us, and all of us are standing in that queue, wanting—no, desperately needing—to be acknowledged as living, unique human beings.

Thanks in large part to the sheer volume of books published, the proliferation of creative writing programs and the attendant demand to publish (anything), along with the entertainment culture described earlier, we now have a kind of literary perpetual-motion machine. Writers are influenced by, among other things, what they read, and if fiction "empty of magic" is what publishers and literary magazines are publishing, their imprimatur becomes a powerful incentive to produce more of the same. The dominant mode, in English and North American fiction, is realism, especially domestic realism, and the anointing of Alice Munro as its high priestess is taken as further evidence that this focus on the world of the self is what readers want. Yet in a recent review of Munro's work, the American novelist Lydia Millet says, "It may be worth asking whether, *in a culture where mainstream society is already wholly consecrated to the worship of self, literary culture should be consecrated to the same faith*" [emphasis added].

II. THE ERASURE OF THE WORLD

According to the American novelist and teacher Janet Burroway, "The history of Western literature shows a movement downward and inward: downward through society from royalty to gentry to the middle classes to the lower classes to the dropouts; inward from heroic action to social drama to individual consciousness to the subconscious to the unconscious." The problem now is that we have nowhere further to go. The result, as a number of contemporary writers are pointing out, is inertia, decay, and irrelevance. We really do not need more short stories and novels in which writers write about writing, or about dysfunctional families, or about individual angst, or about a cache of letters found in an attic revealing X, or about a three-generation family saga—all written in so-called realist mode, sometimes with heavy irony to show that we needn't really invest, or be emotionally moved by, any of this.

In obeisance to modernism, many writers seem to labour under the belief that our complex society is beyond their powers to depict, that all they can offer readers is another small, anemic world. As a result, too much contemporary fiction has no resonance beyond the immediate lives of the characters. Domestic and domesticated, it's tame stuff that fails to challenge its readers' middle-class assumptions and lifestyles. Characters are often depicted in a void, as though the world outside didn't exist—a kind of eternal present in which history, context, depth are all sacrificed to surface. (Such writing appears to be the authors' interpretations of what Hemingway was up to.) Characters also tend to ruminate rather than act, though characters' heads are static and airless places to be for any length of time, especially when the reflections are familiar ones. This fatal combination of lack of action, reliance on generic description, and what I've come to think of as "presentism"—often further constrained by that most limiting of points of view, the first person—results in deadened and deadening prose. We are either being lulled by feel-good stories (anything by Gail Anderson-Dargatz) or titillated by the dirty realism of, for example, Heather McNeil's *Lullabies for Little Criminals*. Yet as the British visual artists Billy Childish and Charles Thomson, founders of the Remodernist movement, remark: "Contemporary writing is cowardly and unchallenging because squalor is tedious, not remarkable. If you find yourself in a rubbish bin, the only interesting narrative is how to climb out, not how ill you can make yourself by ingesting it." (The Remodernists, by the way, claim in their manifesto to be "tak[ing] the original principles of Modernism and reapply[ing] them, highlighting vision as opposed to formalism." Such an approach, they believe, "brings to an end an age of scientific materialism, nihilism and spiritual bankruptcy.")

The downward and inward trend of contemporary fiction is also critiqued by writer Alain de Botton, who remarks on the notable lack of novels about work. "It used to be a central ambition of novelists to capture the experience of working life," he says, "yet writers seem to be losing their nerve." The reasons, he maintains, are writers' lack of experience outside academia and casual jobs, but more importantly, because of "the lack of obvious heroism or romanticism involved in white-collar office work." He adds: "We are now as imaginatively disconnected from the production and distribution of our goods as we are practically in reach of them, a process of alienation which has stripped us of opportunities for wonder, gratitude and guilt." Lydia Millet, in her review of Munro, poses a question that extends the range of de Botton's critique: "Why ... this insistent choice on the purely personal, the proximate world of the self and its near relations? ... Surely the vast universe beyond the minutely personal is also of some little interest."

And therein, I think, lies the problem—the lack of reflection, in much of today's fiction, of "the vast universe beyond the minutely personal." Admittedly there's often a lag in finding contemporary reality explored in fiction, but it's puzzling not to find more writers writing about—oh, a female Member of Parliament, for example, or an outdoor guide witnessing climate change in an Inuit village, or a dancer working in a refugee camp in Namibia. Couldn't we, for awhile, move out of the bedroom, the living room, the mall? What about a fishing boat, an animal shelter, a mining camp? Alain de Botton complains that the working world has dropped off the literary map, noting that the proverbial alien reading contemporary literature "would come away thinking that we devote ourselves almost exclusively to leading complex relationships, squabbling with our parents and occasionally murdering people."

It's not just a question of setting; it's also a matter of giving characters depth, of portraying them as shaped by their past experience, of bringing other, broader worlds to life. To quote Millet again: "The problems [in Munro's fiction] are rarely starvation or war; they tend to be adultery or career disappointment, say, which leaves us with a literary culture whose preoccupation is not meaning or beauty, not right or wrong, not our philosophies or propensity for atrocities or corrupt churches and governments, but rather our sex lives, our social mistakes, our neighborhood failures and sibling rivalries."

This isn't, needless to say, an argument for a wholesale return to nineteenth-century-style realism, *a la* Rohinton Mistry, or to argue that fiction's role is simply to mirror outer reality. It's a call to open up those airless rooms to let in the multiplicity of outside experience and meaning, to return to a fiction that's subversive, transgressive, unsettling. It's instructive, in this context, to compare Munro with Mavis Gallant, who worked as a journalist in the forties in Montreal, left at age twenty-eight for Paris, and lived the rest of her life in Europe. Unlike Munro, Gallant's stories almost always show us how the personal lives of her characters are shaped by offstage political and historical events. Her characters move within complex layerings of space and time, often only half-aware of these external, impersonal forces. It's these stories, for me at least, that now seem more resonant, that provide a more universal echo, given the increasing darkness of our age and the fact that most of us are exiles of one kind or another.

In an article in *Mother Jones* in 2010, the editor of the *Virginia Quarterly Review*, Ted Genoways, deplored the fact that American writers (and by extension Canadian) had forgotten how to write about big issues. "The less commercially viable fiction became, the less it seemed to concern itself with its audience, which in turn made it less commercial, until, like a dying star, it seems on the verge of implosion. Indeed, most American writers seem to have forgotten how to write about big issues—as if giving two shits about the world has gotten crushed under the boot sole of postmodernism. In this vacuum, nonfiction has experienced a renaissance ..." His article ends with a *cri de coeur*: "... [W]riters need to venture out from under the protective wing of academia, to put themselves and their work on the line. Stop being so damned dainty and polite. Treat writing like your lifeblood instead of your livelihood. And for Christ's sake, write something we might want to read."

III. THE FAILURE OF IMAGINATION

An unidentified American blogger in the *Guardian* books section, a few years ago, talked about the "puritanical distrust of imagination" afflicting writers of his—or her?—generation. All the most vital writers, he claimed, are patrolling "what Michael Chabon has called 'the borderlands' between the settled metropolis of realism and genre's wild frontiers." He quoted from Ursula Le Guin's essay "Why Are Americans Afraid of Dragons?" in which she notes that many Americans, especially men, "have learned to repress their imagination, to reject it as something childish or effeminate, unprofitable, and probably sinful." (Which is no doubt part of the reason why so many male American writers have been alcoholics—but that's another essay.) Such fear, I think, applies to Canadians, too, who after all inherited a fairly dour, Calvinist tradition from the Scots who arrived in Canada as homesteaders, fur traders, and explorers. That may also provide a partial explanation for why many men, if they read at all, prefer nonfiction to fiction.

This distrust of the imagination has led to the dominance of realism in contemporary Canadian—indeed most English—fiction. Realist novels are, of course, simulacra of life, not actual reality. Yet an insistence on so-called realism limits our imaginative universes, helping to produce yet more of those airless indoor novels with largely domestic settings. In an imaginary dialogue in his essay "The Dragon's Grandmother," G.K. Chesterton argues against realism: "Can you not see that fairy tales in their essence are quite solid and straightforward; but that this everlasting fiction about modern life is in its nature essentially incredible? Folk lore means that the soul is sane, but the universe is wild and full of marvels. Realism means that the world is dull and full of routine, but that the soul is sick and screaming." Chesterton goes on: "In the fairy tales the cosmos goes mad; but the hero does not go mad. In the modern novels the hero is mad before the book begins, and suffers from the harsh steadiness and cruel sanity of the cosmos."

"In the fairy tales the cosmos goes mad ..."—perhaps that tiny phrase succinctly explains why "fairy tales"—fantasy—now speak more and more to our times. The cosmos has gone mad, in all spheres. Faced with such madness, readers understandably want

stories that help to make sense of the madness, that help them make sense of and confront it. A story like *Lord of the Rings*, where three stand-ins for vulnerable and weak humans must confront the powers of darkness, speaks to our time in a way that no fully realistic novel can. Young adult writers, like Lois Lowry, whose marvellous fable-like novel *The Giver* depicts a highly controlled society where unwanted children are killed, likewise confront the existence of darkness head on. It's not surprising, then, that many adults are reading young-adult fiction, and writers like Neil Gaiman and Suzanne Collins (*The Hunger Games*) and up on adult bestseller lists. Canada, too, is producing strong young adult fantasy writers—Kenneth Oppel, Arthur Slade, Kelley Armstrong.

Speculative fiction for adults is also gaining ground. One reason is that fantasy (as all fiction should) makes a larger world explicit. World-building is what today's best speculative fiction does, and most of it no longer takes place on a distant planet. British writer China Miéville's *The City & the City*, to take one example, imagines an alternate pair of cities called Beszel and Ul Qoma where citizens of one are forbidden to look at the other, even though the two cities are physically intertwined—or are they? Miéville's portrait evokes quantum weirdness, reflecting (far more accurately than most contemporary literary fiction) its impossible-to-grasp reality. (Physicist Richard Feynman famously said: "I think I can safely say that nobody understands quantum mechanics.") The setting of the novel functions rather like a verbal Escher painting, continually upending our conception of it. Yet the story itself is a fairly conventional noir detective mystery involving a murdered academic and her search for a mysterious third city that may—or may not—exist between the other two.

Fantasy fiction also raises the stakes, thereby continuing an ancient literary tradition. Certainly much fantasy traces the journey of the protagonist who must undergo immense trials of one kind or another, echoing not only Shakespeare and the classical Greek tragedians but life itself. Such fiction depicts a self that is active in a world, not merely a self in relation to other selves. That focus on relationships is why contemporary literary fiction often fails to interest men and why, rightly or wrongly, it has gained a reputation as being written primarily for women. Women writers themselves often seem to limit their writing to the domestic arena—once a radical choice—even though women today, at least in the West, have more access to the world than ever. One of the judges of the Orange Prize for women's fiction in 2007, journalist Muriel Gray, deplored the lack of inventiveness and imagination among the submissions. "It's hard to ignore the sheer volume of thinly disguised autobiographical writing from women on small-scale domestic themes such as motherhood, boyfriend troubles and tiny family dramas. These writers appear to have forgotten the fundamental imperative of fiction writing. It's called making stuff up."

The fundamental imperative of fiction writing—odd that we need reminding. Yet our need for story—imaginative, original, spellbinding—seems to be innate. "Readers had been abandoned—they wanted stories," says the Spanish novelist Arturo Pérez-Reverte, explaining that when he started out as a writer he was told that "you had to write intimately, with no action and no characters—the typical book about the self. None of the books that were being published at the time have survived." French novelist Jean-Pierre Ohl says the same thing, confessing that he reads very little contemporary French fiction "because it bores me…

125

talking about things that happened in your own little life—who'd cheated on you, in Paris, in the sixth arrondissement." Strictly realist writers, he adds, "interest me less than *those who unlock the imagination* [emphasis mine]."

IV. THE NEED FOR RE-ENCHANTMENT

We were the sane, the rational, the dreamless people...
—Thomas Berry

We like to think we are sane and rational, but in fact we live under a terrible enchantment—that of the machine. "What we seem unwilling or unable to recognize," says the late theologian and cosmologist Thomas Berry, "is that our entire modern world is itself inspired not by any rational process, but by a distorted dream experience, perhaps by the most powerful dream that has ever taken possession of human imagination [that of technology] … The difficulty of our times is our inability to awaken out of this cultural pathology." Robert Bringhurst, the renowned poet and Haida translator, says that we live in a world he describes as "synthetic, self-absorbed, and unsustainable." Why "synthetic"? Because we believe that the technological world we have created is the real one, that we can live divorced from our origins in the natural world. The theologian and philosopher Diarmuid O'Murchu speaks of our "cultural death wish," noting that "when the arts themselves succumb to the morbidity and inertia of a dwindling culture, then what is left to project us toward new meaning?" We have, in fact, delegated dreaming to a caste of artists, but their dreaming in a commodified world cannot help us.

Where are the writers who, recognizing our plight, are casting the spells of different stories? Those writers patrolling Michael

Chabon's "borderlands" explicitly rejecting the dominant literary mode in favour of a more hybrid and adventurous approach, including Chabon himself? In a 2002 essay Chabon decried the state of modern short fiction (including his own), which with rare exceptions consisted slely of "the contemporary, quotidian, plotless, moment-of-truth revelatory story...sparkling with epiphanic dew." Chabon's novel *The Amazing Adventures of Kavalier and Clay* was the first speculative tinged fiction to win the Pulitzer Prize (in 2001), while his more recent *The Yiddish Policeman's Union* is a hilarious and poignant alternative-history-plus-noir-detective novel in which the Jews of Europe find refuge in Alaska during the Second World War. (The U.S. Secretary of the Interior at the time, Harold L. Ickes, actually proposed such a rescue plan, thereby demonstrating that the border between fantasy and reality is far less firmly patrolled in real life.)

Other American writers blurring the boundary between literary and speculative fiction include Kelly Link (*Magic for Beginners*), Karen Russell (*St. Lucy's Home for Girls Raised by Wolves*), and Kevin Brockmeier (*A Brief History of the Dead*). Several recent short story anthologies of what has variously been called "slipstream," "interstitial," or—to borrow a term invented by Chabon—"Trickster literature" have appeared too. "This is literature in mid-transformation," the American critic and writer Lev Grossman said prophetically in a 2004 article in *Time* magazine, "the modernist bleeding into the postmodern and beyond ... [Y]ou can almost see the future of literature coming." This future, of course, is part of the past in countries where writers, having borne witness (often with their bodies) to the oppression dn corruption under which they lived, produced works such as Mikhail Bulgakov's satiric

Faustian fantasy *The Master and Margarita*, Bruno Schulz's *Sanatorium Under the Sign of the Hourglass* and Jose Saramago's *A Year in the Death of Ricardo Reis*. When reality is fantastical, perhaps only explicitly: "I write fantasy because the reality I see around me is fantastical, so that fantasy becomes a new realism, representing our reality, the reality of the twenty-first century, more accurately the old realism, which was formed in the nineteenth ... [R]ealism is also an ideology, one that can obscure reality as much as it can illuminate it ... It is fantasy that allows us to imagine the world we want to create."

Canada, as usual, is trailing behind, although francophone writers have always been more at home with the magical and mystical (perhaps influenced by the Québécois tradition of the folktale). Among anglo writers there is Margaret Atwood's recent dystopian fiction (which some might categorize as straightforward science fiction); Sheila Heti, with her miniature tales, Stephen Marche's Borgesian contribution, *Shining at the Bottom of the Sea*, a literary anthology from an imagined country; and Thomas King, who draws on the archetypal figures of First Nations stories. The recent anthology *Darwin's Bastards* suggests that Canada might be finally catching up, though borderlands fiction has yet to make it onto any Canadian literary prize lists.

"The Age of Separation is the result of the story we have built, a story we tell ourselves about ourselves," says the writer Charles Eisenstein. "We have told and retold and endlessly elaborated the story of Separation. Now it is time to tell a different one." What might that new meta-story be? Instead of perpetuating a dying paradigm, its stories will function as harbingers and intimations of a new one. The energy to do so will come from the planet itself, from the natural world of which we are an inseparable part. "The earth is, and always has been, a depth repository of the mythic," says writer and environmentalist Stephen Harrod Buhner. "We need to re-establish our connection with the mythic, to allow our stories to be imbued with that level of reality, if we are to renew ourselves, our stories, and our world."

Even scientist are among those calling for a new narrative. The discovery that fourteen billion years of cosmological evolution preceded us, says the mathematical cosmologist Brian Swimme, is as potentially shattering as Copernicus' finding that the earth wasn't stationary but revolved around the sun. "We are enveloped by a self-organizing community that is another form of intelligence, "Swimme says, adding that "our new challenge is to reinvent our civilization." Reductionist science, in other words, is no longer adequate for telling the story of our universe and ourselves. Swimme's own one-line version of this story is both poetic and mythic: "You take hydrogen gas, and you leave it alone, and it turns into rosebuds, giraffes, and humans."

In his remarkable essay "The Arts and Planetary Survival," Denys Trussell argues that all serious artists are now faced with a struggle to 'ensoul' their work," thereby restoring the sacramental basis of society that machine culture destroyed. "Art inevitably implies or embodies a cosmology," says Trussell, adding that "if we take the concept of the earth as a great self-regulating entity, we have meaning. It means something that such a huge entity can be seen as a resplendent and unified process. It affirms something in us, who must also maintain ourselves as stable and unified creatures." One of the vital tasks of literature is to cleanse the web of consciousness that covers the planet—what the French philosopher-priest and paleontologist Pierre Teilhard de Chardin called the "noosphere"—of spiritual pollution, venality and the lies of economism." Such work, Trussell acknowledges, cannot overthrow the false gods of economism alone, "but at least art can act through its ancient mimetic *role in prefiguring and dramatizing their overthrow* [emphasis mine]."

Helping to dismantle the current world view by showing that it is not inevitable—not in fact "real"—is a revolutionary act. We need stories in which the stakes matter, in which we are not mere individuals, or families, or even communities but participants in a vast web of being. We need stories that incorporate some of the wildness, the strangeness, the mystery of the world around us. Giving voice to other perceptions, other forms of being, that might help to heal the split between humanity and the natural world. "The day is not far distant," says Teilhard de Chardin, "when humanity will realize that biologically it is faced with a choice between suicide and adoration." We are on the brink of that precipice now. The young activists of the Arab and north African revolts, and now those of the occupy movement, are showing us imagination in action. As writers we, too, must revivify old forms by using our imaginations in the service of old stories. In doing so we can reclaim the essential role of the storyteller, the one who reminds us who we are and where we came from, and who restores the world through authentic story.

Brand Me

Maryam Sanati

In the competitive field of personal branding, Gregory Gorgeous is considered a champ. His vlogs (like blogs, but with video), which consist mainly of cosmetics tutorials, have generated 25.6 million YouTube views, presumably by people who want to look like a Real Housewife of Orange County. I've watched the tilt of his Carol Brady hairdo and the gloss of his Kristen Stewart lips as he offers a lesson on thermal hair spray. "Stay gorgeous!" he says. I've also witnessed his account of the night he lost his iPhone in a club, a story that wends, for eight unbearable minutes, along a road to nowhere. Weakly leveraging the "born this way" message of the times, he makes paid and unpaid endorsements (though there's never any distinction) for his "favourite things," such as sparkly fuchsia platform pumps and a line called Swedish Skin, in his videos and on *officialgregorygorgeous.com*.

One of the countless young Canadians seeking fame and fortune in "lifestyle blogging," Gorgeous kick-started his YouTube semi-celebrity as a bored sixteen-year-old in 2008, then followed a well-worn path to semi-riches: launch a YouTube channel, tweet about yourself (he counts more than 48,000 followers), secure sponsorship from advertisers, bask in the attention. He is part of a digital black hole that's sucking up the most superficial minds of his generation, including a phalanx of aspiring PR girls who spend all day photographing themselves, a fraternity of party-hearty amateur rappers who hoist red plastic cups in a kind of ne'er-do-well salute, and platinum blondes who go by names like Raymi the Minx, and Lauren O'Nizzle (real name: O'Neil). On *Lauren Out Loud*, the latter blogs about dyeing her cat's tail green, and her love of "kitty-cat videos"; this recent *Toronto Star* intern is now qualified to be, in her words, an "instructor of online journalism at a local college." At twenty-six, she has a modest 6,200 Twitter followers, but she is a leading Blondebot (also her word) of the personal blogging scene, with a creative signature that does little more than establish how cute she looks in a tank top.

Gorgeous and O'Nizzle are only two of the attention-seeking asteroids careening through the universe of personal branding. What these kids have in common is a goal: to become a new order of quasi-socialite. What they stand for, sadly, is nothing.

This alone should irk the hell out of anyone who is older than they are, and it frequently does, particularly the glib fortysomethings of my peer group, who revel in damning shallowness. My people also profess to distrust all conspicuous self-promoters. So we can find no better target for our ire than kids who self-promote without so much as a product to sell.

But I've learned a few things about this axe we're grinding: First, that protesting their inanity on the Internet is as futile as spearfishing with a toothpick. Second, that lifestyle bloggers haven't cornered the market on being inane. And finally, that they weren't just "born this way." Okay—they were. But all little monsters were spawned by something. And that particular something is my Gen X. That's right—it's kind of our fault.

Grown-ups, here are the harsh tokes: We are the ones who made brands out of every nostalgic pop culture totem from Tootsie Rolls to Beavis and Butt-Head. We are the ones who started the irrational obsession with the concept of branding, by reading our copies of *No Logo* and lobbying for bike lanes while driving our Subaru to Starbucks. (It's embarrassing when the worst cliché about your peer group is actually true.) We are a generation of both thumb-twiddling and eye-gouging ambition, who spent half of the '90s resenting the boomers—for soaking up all of the riches and leaving us the scraps—and the other half thrashing around in the deep end of online enterprise.

Our resulting self-obsession encouraged the Millennials' worst narcissism, yet still we scoff.

By many accounts, the concept of the personal brand was first introduced by marketers Al Ries and Jack Trout (both my parents' age, as it turns out), with their 1987 book, *Positioning: The Battle for Your Mind*, in which they advise corporate cogs to use a "positioning strategy to advance your own career." I was in my twenties when that notion received a major public airing, in a 1997 article in *Fast Company*, then a new business magazine with its lens tightly focused on tech-driven start-ups. The dot-com universe was booming with overvalued companies that would soon implode, and although most of us didn't have a clue what the Internet meant, we hoped it would result in gainful employment. The author of the *Fast Company* piece, management thinker Tom Peters (or "tompeters!" as he brands himself) exhorted readers to develop an indelible mark, like the Nike swoosh or the Starbucks siren. "It's time for me—and you," he wrote, "—to take a lesson from the big brands, a lesson that's true for anyone who's interested in what it takes to stand out and prosper in the new world of work." Today his essay reads like Orwellian fiction, an eager fist pump for the commodification of the self. As for the locus of branding's next boom, Peters identified the Internet.

The tech boom was about young people propelling themselves into the future, but unfortunately we were conditioned to our very core to wait our turn—for a tap on the shoulder that meant we could join the boomers in the traditional job market. Waiting had become a way of life; fearing unknown consequences, we practically invented putting things off. So our response to Peters' call to arms was conflicted. First, inspiration ("I have to figure out my brand"), followed by panic ("I have to figure out my brand!"), followed by embittered defiance ("Who needs a bloody brand anyway?").

In the decades after the *Fast Company* story, we became further discouraged by fear of failure: as people, at work, and eventually as parents. Instead of doing things, we jabbered on about our lives to anyone who would listen, voicing our "takes" more than any previous generation had, a penchant that gave birth to a ubiquitous breed of personal, confessional writing, from "young gal in the big city" columns in print to "young mom coping with Chardonnay" blogs online.

When a new generation appeared on the scene, with new media at their fingertips—and brimming with self-esteem, thanks to their poor, well-intentioned parents—they deftly realized the concepts we struggled to wrap our heads around. The supersize personas that emerged, kids who were self-assured and style obsessed, invited damning generalizations. But I'm looking for reasons to understand the monstrosities we created, and maybe even to cut them a little slack.

Toronto's Casie Stewart is a pixie blonde with an ardent audience—50,000 unique visitors to her blog, *This Is My Life*, and a Twitter following of over 7,000—that consists of sixty percent young girls. That crowd, she says, tells her all the time how much she inspires them to be "positive" individuals whose purpose is to enjoy "the VIP life." This entails attending openings and junkets, and promoting products (be they Puma shoes or Virgin America flights), often in return for free stuff. Air New Zealand recently sent Stewart to cover its fashion week, where she drank in the experience of riding around with a car and driver. When we meet, just after the Halloween weekend, she tells me she spent the day working at her friend's vintage fashion store in downtown Toronto, in exchange for free clothes.

Stewart seems sunny and rather sweet, a twenty-nine-year-old who blogs about going to the gym, hanging out with her friends, and sunbathing topless—though she says she prefers not to "show my boobs" as others in her peer group do, "because my mom reads my blog." (In her teens, she posed in a not-so-fashionable bikini as a Sunshine Girl in the *Toronto Sun*.) When I check Klout, a company that "identifies influencers on topics across the social web," I find her score is a healthy fifty-eight out of one-hundred. The Klout score is an entirely scary invention that quantifies registrants' ubiquity and audience reach by looking at their social media profiles and interactions. Gregory Gorgeous ranks a sixty-one. Lauren O'Nizzle, a friend and digital soulmate of Stewart's, scores a sixty-three. Kim Kardashian's hovers around ninety-two.

I see where Stewart is coming from. For someone with small-town roots (Cambridge, Ontario), living large in the big city of Toronto is a thrill. She runs her personal brand as a full-time job, having been fired from a marketing position at Much mtv for excessive blogging on the job. She employs a paid intern, and has managed to climb out of a tuition-fuelled $30,000 debt through an appearance on the W Network's financial makeover show, *Maxed Out*. She now makes bank by speaking to companies about ramping up their social media strategies.

"The brand," she says, "is bigger than me now." When she describes how she built it, I'm reminded of an interview I read with marketer Hubert Rampersad, author of the bestseller *Authentic Personal Branding: A New Blueprint for Building and Aligning a Powerful Leadership Brand*, part of a recent pack of books instructing us all to self-market. Branding, he writes, is about controlling the impression people have of you, and making that impression desirable (which is not, of course, the cakewalk these authors make it out to be). Building an authentic personal brand is a way of "improving yourself continuously." Though we're obsessive about improvement, my generation might feel almost as embarrassed touting Rampersad's advice as we would be donning folk costumes and dancing the mazurka. But because Stewart's peers have not known self-doubt as much as we have, and because they're so much better at manoeuvring in the digital age than we were, they feel perfectly at ease. "I think to myself," Stewart says, "that I created all this by putting out positive thoughts and accepting things into my life. I dreamt about doing this—getting the star treatment—and now I am."

Sidling up to every willing PR agent, then, is a Millennial way to present the authentic self, about as awkward and disingenuous as New Age was thirty years ago. Yet Stewart seems blissfully, radiantly, ear-to-ear happy.

But not everyone finds their bliss in doing dumb stuff: not style and society blogger Nolan Bryant, who is about to turn twenty. Though his mini-fame resulted from his smart use of digital resources, he is nothing like Casie Stewart. For him, the star treatment is a beast of a different stripe. A follower of fashion since childhood, he is known for his long hair and his six-foot-five stature, and for wearing capes. Those who follow his personal brand assume he comes from money. In truth, like the Factory crew orbiting Andy Warhol, or Truman Capote orbiting Babe Paley and Slim Keith, he is enthralled with the rich and famous. His budding career is as a social chronicler/new media socialite, and he's good at it.

Another small-town kid (from Newcastle, Ontario), Bryant belongs to a WASP family, he says, but not a society one. His father worked in corporate communications, promoting hotels for Fairmont. As a boy of six, he would find himself sitting rapt in the Library Bar of the Royal York Hotel. "I believe the socially affluent in Toronto to be fascinating," he says, paraphrasing a Herb Caen quote about "cockroaches and socialites being the only things that can stay up all night and eat anything."

Bryant began attending Toronto Fashion Week shows when he was in grade nine, via an aunt who worked at CBC and had a connection to the television show *Fashion File*. That was the era, he says, when "everyone worked in magazines or was a buyer." Now, he observes, "everyone is a blogger. Everyone has a Twitter account. So many of them hang around outside at fashion shows, taking pictures of people in weird outfits. That's not for me." He had bigger aspirations. Through a friendship with Marissa Bronfman (of the Seagram Bronfmans), whom he met at Fashion Week, he became well known to the right PR people, was photographed for the party pages, and found himself in the front rows alongside the reed-thin elite. He took their pictures, which provided much of the content for *nolanbryant.com*, which he launched in 2008. The exposure brought him attention, including an invitation by Hugo Boss to shoot the company's collection at Berlin Fashion Week in 2010.

When we meet for coffee, I find it remarkable that he is only nineteen; he is so self-confident and measured. "I wear the fun clothes, I blog about it, and I socialize," he says when I ask him to describe what defines his personal brand. He also understands the line between self-promotion and exploitation. "When you're photographed by the party pages, they always list your name and where you work. In the beginning, it was just my name. I wanted to go to events and have something else people could say about me."

What he was really doing, like so many others, was looking for a way to present his identity—which is, in the end, the purpose of youth. It's just that he started with a baseline the teenagers of my era lacked. As well as the digital tools, he possessed an uncannily solid sense of himself. Like all socialites on the ascent, confidence became his key. His generation lives out life in public; my generation chose to lurk in the shadows, scared shitless about what others thought of us. To paraphrase Henry Rollins, we spent half of our lives screwing up, and the other half making up for it. Bryant and his peers strode purposefully out of the gate. This, at the very least, is admirable.

I find no new media arriviste more sure of herself than Sarah Nicole Prickett, a brand who craves some distance from the Blonde-bots of the world. She doesn't consider herself a style blogger, although she blogs about style (and happens to be blond). That label would put her in the wider concentric circle of online personalities whose ambitions are shallow, whose observations are generic, and whose writing is poor.

Meanwhile, she struggles with a few categories of her own. "I'm a Millennial, right?" she asks me. "I keep reading about how unhappy we supposedly are." One such piece happens to appear on the cover of *New York* magazine the week she and I meet in a downtown Toronto restaurant called the Böhemian Gastropub. (When she points out how awful the name is, and I agree, I'm left wondering which of our generations has the bigger compulsion to *comment on everything.*)

The *New York* cover shows a guy I can only describe as an emo—which is probably no longer a Millennially correct designation—shot in black and white and looking nobly tragic. The line across his chest says, "Sucks to Be Us." The story is about children of over-praising parents, kids who grow up to Google Chat and live in angst in Brooklyn. Held up as symbols of "post-hope America," they are described as "screwed, coddled, self-absorbed, mocked," yet "surprisingly resilient."

Many of these adjectives might seem appropriate—but not "screwed." Prickett strikes me as neither unhappy nor disadvantaged. Her red lipstick is too flawless, her five-inch wedge platforms imperially high. By her own account, she is right where she wants to be, and is far more in control of her personal image at twenty-six than I was of mine at thirty-six. She has a career as a freelance writer for the *National Post*, the *Toronto Standard*, and *Fashion* magazine. She confidently calls herself a "good writer." (I wouldn't have had the guts to say that about my own writing at twenty-six—or forty!) And she has something her 5,000 or so Twitter followers consider significant: a growing status as a new media personality and party fixture. Strangers refer to her by the abbreviation

SNP, and when visitors read her site, *snprickett.com*, which has seventeen sections, like a lifestyle magazine, they will assume she is the centre of a magnificent universe. It's more accurate to call her a big fish in the medium-sized pond of Toronto fashion.

Later today, she will attend a charity runway show featuring outfits modelled by dogs. Let that not paint a picture of her erudition. She's reading Haruki Murakami, which she notes on her Twitter feed. On her site, she quotes Baudelaire and writes about Nellie Bly. In person, she is articulate, likeable, and smart. She is also comfortable with public exposure. "Self-promotion used to be reviled," she says, referencing my era. "Kurt Cobain said, 'I don't want to be on MTV,' and then he was on MTV. This was sneakier—pretending you didn't want the attention in order to garner more of it."

But the idea of a brand leaves her uneasy: "People have said that to me, in person at parties. 'You have a great personal brand.' I mean, who says that to someone?" The idea makes her feel so disingenuous that "someone should pull my hair back so I can vomit." That's because her plan was to self-express rather than to self-brand. (If she could write about any subject, she says, it would be "my feelings. But there's not a huge market for that.") She was raised in London, Ontario, with four younger siblings, by deeply religious parents: "We went to church five times a week. I didn't have a computer until I was ten, and no Internet until sixteen. My parents didn't like popular or secular culture. You read the Brontës but didn't read *The Baby-Sitters Club*."

As a form of rebellion, she began buying fashion magazines and writing an online journal. After she moved to Toronto, the whole thing grew, aided and abetted by her apparent enjoyment at having her picture taken and broadcasting her thoughts. To illustrate the generational divide I'm feeling when I listen to her, my friends and I would find putting our faces, clothes, hair, makeup, boots, penchants, partners, and reading lists out into the world terrifying.

I don't want to moan over Gen X's lot in life, as we have nothing to feel sorry for. My peers are educated and successful, own property, and are usually pleasant to be around. However, many of us grew up feeling like hapless bystanders to the extraordinary events of our time. Over the years, we honed a diagnostic, eyebrow-raising pose on the sidelines, but it's just a cloaking mechanism for our own insecurities. In the end, my anxious group's greatest setback might be our dread of any scrutiny or derision; maybe that's why we scrutinize others and sit in judgment ourselves. I'm now in a position of envy: neither Prickett nor any of her peers, frivolous or thoughtful, boob flashing or not, suffers from that growth-stunting trepidation.

"I just thought," she tells me, reflecting on the plans she made in her youth, "who do I want to be?" Her decision was: "I can make myself. I have all the resources here in this city at my disposal. And now, when girls like the one I used to be—shy, sheltered girls from small towns—write to me and say I helped them understand something, or they don't feel as weird now, or that they want to move to the city to have my life, even though I understand that my life is kind of bullshit, I think that's good. I needed people like that when I was young."

The rest of us, the elders of the kind who swore never to join Facebook or Twitter (and then did), are only now, through gritted teeth, starting to ask the question.

What's my personal brand?

I haven't the foggiest.

On Tipping in Cuba

Chris Turner

More than a million Canadians will travel to Cuba this year. The only places beyond our borders that attract more of us are the United States and Mexico. There is no other tourist destination on earth where Canadians are so dominant, and possibly none where the tourist economy is more vital to the nation's immediate economic health. With little in the way of formal policy and with no real intent on the part of the beach-bound hordes, we've established a relationship with Cuba that is unique in both our histories. We've colonized Cuba on vacation by accident.

This is a story about what happens when the unarticulated, half-hidden nature of that colonial relationship is suddenly exposed. It's an economics lesson in the form of a parable, a traveller's tale about the strange connection between master and servant in this de facto tourist colony.

So let's begin, in fairy-tale fashion, in a tower atop a castle: the rooftop terrace of Hotel Casa Granda in Santiago de Cuba, the country's second-largest city. The Casa Granda is an old colonial half ruin overlooking a wide square and an elegant cathedral. It's an atmospheric, Graham Greene kind of place, five storeys tall and colonnaded and shedding white paint. I found myself there at sunset one January evening, sipping a mojito and pondering the real value of ten convertible Cuban pesos.

Because Cuba is among the few nations on earth with two official currencies, a never-never-land economy caught in its own distended bubble halfway between the collapsed Soviet bloc and the contemporary global capitalist order, visitors can find themselves wondering more than usual about exchange rates. There is the regular, nonconvertible peso, officially the Cuban peso or CUP, used to buy staple goods at state-run shops. And there is the convertible peso, the CUC—the hard currency, which is used for luxury goods and provides the default banknotes for the tourist economy. In government accounting, CUCs and CUPs are valued one to one, but informally the CUC is worth about the same as the Canadian dollar, while the CUP has a street value of a nickel at most. CUPs are worthless outside Cuba, except as souvenirs.

Earlier in the day, I'd had ten CUCs snatched from my hand, and I was up on the roof of the Casa Granda trying to figure out what exactly had happened and how I really felt about it. It's rare, once you're well into the mortgage-and-kids phase of adulthood, to encounter a whole new category of emotion, but I was pretty sure I'd done just that out there on a dusty Santiago back street, and now I was probing the feeling to discern its dimensions.

What happened, in brief, is that my wife and I had hired a young man named Antonio to give us a tour. We'd spent the morning chugging around in an ancient Moskvich sedan, with another young man driving as Antonio pointed out the sights and delivered a running commentary about what he called "the reality of Cuba." We'd visited an Afro-Cuban cultural museum, toured the old Spanish fort, bought contraband rum. We'd gone back to Antonio's tiny concrete box of a home, met his wife and mother, sipped beers, talked some politics, and taken pictures. In the late afternoon, he and another friend had led us to a lovely little restaurant at the base of Santiago's landmark Padre Pico steps. We'd eaten grilled lobster, drunk more beers, and traded jokes and vows of eternal friendship.

At the end of the meal, I'd given the waiter CUC $80 and received CUC $10 in change, and as I stood there with the ten-peso note in my hand Antonio grabbed and pocketed it. I shot him a confused look, and he responded with a half shrug that seemed calibrated somewhere between *What's it matter?* and *You know the score.* I hadn't intended to give him the money, but he decided he deserved it. Hours later, on the rooftop patio of the Casa Granda, drinking a mojito that cost nearly half the amount I was obsessing about, I wondered what that shrug really meant.

This had all occurred in that informal, sketchily delineated commercial zone that springs up in pretty much any robust tourist economy, a grey market that is particularly broad and heavily trafficked in countries where visitors and locals are separated by wide gulfs of wealth, power, or political freedom. In Cuba, Antonio and I stood on opposite sides of a divide created by a substantial admixture of all three.

We were under no illusions, my wife and I. We understood that Antonio was, in local parlance, a *jinetero*—a tout or fixer, though in Cuba the word often suggests a darker meaning: hustler or scam artist. We'd participated in a drawn-out haggling courtship with him across a couple of days, a dance familiar to us from other trips to countries with bustling grey markets. There had been repeated encounters on a busy street in front of a tiny, decrepit photo studio that may or may not have been his usual place of work. He'd presented us with a gift of a photo and some cheap cigars, and we'd discussed the possibility of a city tour as if it were a friendly outing and not a paid transaction. We'd checked with the tour desk of the Meliá hotel, the only full-service resort in town, and knew that an organized tour in an air-conditioned bus would run us more than $100. We preferred the idea of giving our hard-currency CUCs and maybe a gift or two to an enterprising *jinetero* instead of to a government controlled joint venture.

It was the right choice, and we had no regrets. It had been a fun day, revelatory in ways an official tour never could have been, and we'd been generous with Antonio and his family, paying out his fee in bits and pieces, in overpayments and unasked-for change. I'd overpaid for drinks at the Afro-Cuban cultural centre, handed him too much money by a factor of at least five to pick up a six-pack of beer to share back at his house. We'd stopped back at our hotel at the end of the tour and filled a bag for him and his family with markers, notebooks, two toothbrushes, some new towels, and a used pair of Adidas shorts. We'd paid him and the driver CUC $20 each for their work as guides—the equivalent of a month's wages in a typical government job—and had bought him and his other friend lobster dinners (another month's wages, although the place never would've served Cuban diners on their own, even if they'd had the CUCs).

So, yes: we all knew roughly what the score was. But to Antonio's mind, I'd come up with a figure at least CUC $10 too low, and he'd taken it upon himself to round it up. At first, standing in the street outside the restaurant as he and his friend departed in a flurry of hugs and warm handshakes, I'd felt something verging on a sense of violation. Had I been robbed? Had I been—that most dreaded of veteran traveller fears—played somehow? Was I a sucker?

With the clarity of a second mojito and the brilliant sunset over Santiago Bay, I knew that wasn't it. This wasn't a robbery or a con. This is why it felt so weird: it wasn't about what had happened to me; it was about *who I was* in Cuba. This had been a refusal to hew to the script of colonial power. It was a servant's insubordination before his colonial master. It was, I came to think, a profoundly Cuban way to read the situation.

Of course I could spare the ten pesos, and Antonio had earned it and then some. I'd seen just enough to imagine how hard it would be for him to get his hands on another CUC $10 note, and he understood all too well how effortless it was for me to obtain a big stack of them. He wasn't fully invested in the tourist economy's cold logic of wealth and status, and he certainly didn't feel he owed me any deference. He'd simply taken what was rightfully his, an inverted colonial tax on the day's transaction. Quite literally, it was what the market would bear on that particular day in Santiago.

By the time I'd reached the mashed lime and mint leaves at the bottom of my second mojito, I saw the whole thing much more clearly: me and Antonio, Cuba and Canada, the whole trip. The real exchange rate on ten convertible pesos preoccupied me for the rest of our visit and cast new light on the month's preparation leading up to it. Ten pesos was a bargain, really, for all that had been revealed.

A few days before we departed for Cuba, we stopped by the Wal-mart in Antigonish, Nova Scotia, where we were visiting my parents for Christmas. We had pictures to get printed and some final purchases to make in preparation for the trip: sunscreen, medication, a high-capacity memory stick. One of the unspoken assumptions in Canada's colonial relationship with Cuba is that tourists import stockpiles of consumer goods to hand out to locals. In Cuba, unlike the rest of the beach holiday Caribbean, it's not just that people can't afford as much as we can, but that much of what we take for granted is completely unavailable in

Cuba's truncated marketplace. I'd been reading on the Internet about what people suggested to bring: dental floss, shampoo, good towels, baseballs, vitamins and medicines, toothbrushes and school supplies, hardware and reading glasses.

We wandered Wal-Mart's over-lit aisles, past overflowing shelves, filling a cart with pens and notepads and econo-sized bottles of acetaminophen. We had our five-year-old daughter in reluctant tow, and she settled into a shelf piled with towels as if it were a bunk bed while we had an absurd debate about which of them to buy. The towel aisle had at least four distinct gradations of price and quality. I'd written "high-quality towels" on my list and put a big asterisk next to it, but I couldn't remember whether I was reminding myself that towels were so useful we should buy as many as possible or that Cubans needed particularly high-quality towels. In the end, we bought two bath towels ($5 each), four washcloths ($2 each), and two hand towels ($4 each). By the time we reached the checkout, I could no longer remember whether they were higher in the quantity or the quality range. The total bill was $186.82, the equivalent of nine months' average wages in Cuba. We paid with the swipe of a card and a tired shrug.

This, of course, is the way of the Canadian economy nowadays. We're delirious with choice, so completely buried in our own abundance that it inspires reality TV series. Many of us rarely bother with cash; some digital chirrup races at the speed of light from Wal-Mart's till to a server farm representing the bank's vault, and by the time we hit the automatic exit we can't remember whether we paid $176 or $186 for the dead weight filling our cart. You could lose CUC $10 just by forgetting to put back that pack of fancy pencil crayons your kid tossed in while you were distracted.

For all the arbitrary afterthoughts that govern its periphery, Canada's relationship with Cuba, economic and otherwise, is a significant one. Canada and Mexico were the only Western nations that didn't cease diplomatic relations with Cuba during the tense missile crisis years of the early '60s, and Fidel Castro was close enough to Pierre Trudeau that he served as an honorary pallbearer at the former prime minister's funeral in Montreal. In the annals of Canadian diplomacy, there is no other international relationship in which Canada has stood as far apart from the US.

As a reward for our enduring friendship, Canada is probably the second most important economic ally Cuba has after Venezuela, which supplies more than sixty percent of the island's oil. (China exports more stuff to Cuba, but the Chinese don't show up daily by the multiple charter-flight-loads to hand out gifts and pour hundreds of millions of dollars into the Cuban economy.) Cuba is our largest trading partner in the whole of Central America and the Caribbean. We export a range of commodities to Cuba—sulphur, wheat, copper wire—and we are the second largest buyer of Cuban exports, particularly sugar, nickel, fish, citrus fruits, and tobacco. That's over $1 billion in total trade. The Canadian mining company Sherritt International has a huge presence in Cuba, digging up nickel; and Toronto-based Pizza Nova, the only foreign pizza joint in the country, has operated six outlets scattered across the island. Back home, meanwhile, souvenir shops in many Canadian cities feature humidors well stocked with Cuban tobacco products for sale to American tourists. The Cuban cigar has become, in a sense, as Canadian as maple syrup.

The economic view from the other end of this relationship is nowhere near as rosy. Since the collapse of the Soviet Union in the late '80s, Cuba has struggled through a punishing "Special Period" during which its economy has existed in its own isolated socialist limbo: tethered to a failed Communist order, still barred from regular trade with the world's largest economy just 145 kilometres across the sea, desperate for imports and the hard currency to pay for them. As Soviet goods vanished from Cuban pantries in the first years of the Special Period, the average Cuban's calorie intake plummeted by thirty percent, and the local diet has never fully recovered. Cuba remains reliant on imported goods (increasingly, under a special exemption, from the US) for somewhere between sixty and eighty percent of its food. Cubans also switched almost overnight to organic and in some cases pre-industrial forms of local food production; the island has experienced a boom in the production of yokes and plows for use with oxen, for example, among many other austerity measures adopted to weather the Special Period's rough, uncertain seas.

Austerity's limits, though, are now lapping perilously high against the makeshift vessel's sides. Since June 2009, Cuba has operated under emergency energy quotas in a program known as "Save or Die," while the government has been laying off workers, encouraging small business development, and sending so many doctors abroad (as trade in kind for vital commodities such as oil) that there are now nearly twice as many Cubans caring for the sick overseas as there are working on the island.

The government has begun to discuss phasing out subsidies for many staple goods, suggesting that the days are numbered for the ration stores that provide Cubans with much of their daily bread (and rice and beans and milk).

One recent study described Cuba's current approach as "survival economics." The Havana-based dissident blogger Yoani

Sanchez, writing for the *Huffington Post* last August, summed up Cuba's conundrum more eloquently: "We are in transition, something seems to be on the verge of being irreparably broken on this island, but we don't realize it, sunk in the day-to-day and its problems ... we are leaving behind something that seemed to us, at times, eternal."

In the face of this deepening uncertainty, there remains one bright and intensifying light on Cuba's troubled horizon, one safe port amid the Special Period storm: tourism. In 1990, at the dawn of this strange age, Cuba attracted 340,000 tourists; in 2011, it welcomed some 2.5 million. Since the announcement of the Save or Die program, Raúl Castro's government has introduced ninety-nine-year leases for foreign investors, to encourage resort and golf course development; and it has loosened the restrictions on family-run, home-based restaurants (*paladares*) and guest houses (*casas particulares*), to provide more self-employment opportunities in the tourist sector. Meanwhile, one in four of the island's 80,000 government tourist workers has a post-secondary degree. "Right now," writes Sanchez, "the main incentive for those who work in snack bars, restaurants and hotels lies in the possibility of a visiting foreigner leaving them some material gratification." More than a million of those foreigners, forty-four percent of the total, are Canadians. The next-largest share, approximately 175,000, belongs to the British. Tipping, once regarded as counter-revolutionary and beneath the dignity of Cuban patriots, has become their most direct and vital connection to economic stability.

To be a Canadian tourist in Cuba is to be something more than a visitor, more even than a run-of-the-mill mark. It's not just that you're visibly foreign and rich; you're a sort of modern vassal, the only readily accessible emissary of a metropole that has never been seen but is generally understood to be bounteous and benevolent.

Such were the macro-socioeconomic forces at work as we strolled down a broad downtown *avenida* on our first full day in Santiago. The traffic on the road was steady and loud, heavy with ancient GM trucks, diesel-belching Chinese buses, and antique Fords and Cadillacs with multiply rebuilt engines growling under their hoods. We stopped to admire the stunning facade of the Hotel Rex, a glorious art deco and neon relic from Cuba's swinging '50s. The Cuban Revolution was born in Santiago, and this was the hotel where the first Fidelistas stayed the night before their failed 1953 raid on the nearby Moncada Barracks. (Following the attack, Fidel, forced from Cuba for leading the attack, would meet Che Guevara during his Mexican exile, returning a few years later and capturing Santiago in late 1958—the first major victory of the revolutionary war.)

Later that morning, a young man waved to us from a concrete stoop half a storey above street level. He'd noticed my wife's camera and invited us in to see his little photo studio. In his solid but thickly accented English, he introduced himself as Antonio.

The studio was a study in contemporary Cuban improvisation. It was located in the cramped front room of the old house, its walls crumbling and peeling in that signature Special Period way. The only light came from a single bare fluorescent tube mounted horizontally on one wall, its unearthly glare illuminating a threadbare white curtain. The sole piece of photographic equipment was a point-and-shoot digital camera that looked at least five years old and produced pictures several megapixels smaller than the ones taken by a basic smart phone. In Santiago, though, access to any digital camera evidently provided a sufficient foundation for a photography business.

Antonio and a couple of colleagues were taking pictures of a baby girl and her proud parents. Her first birthday party was this coming Saturday, and we were promptly invited to attend. We posed for pictures with the birthday girl and her family, and then they left and Antonio launched into a protracted monologue about the local photo business, Santiago ("the most Caribbean city in Cuba"), and his own Afro-Cuban heritage. He dug out his passport and showed us the visa from a trip he'd taken to Amsterdam a few years earlier. He had a couple of pictures of himself in a toque and a heavy coat in the Dutch winter. He knew a musician, he said, who had toured Canada. His ache for escape was palpable.

We left Antonio with a vague promise to return, perhaps for a tour of "the real Cuba," perhaps for the birthday party. We were under no obligation, and we knew enough to be wary, but we meant it all the same.

It was a glorious day, warm under a gentle sun, and we strolled lazily down a nearby market street, stopping to gawk at the strange array of goods in the government shops. Cheap Chinese shoes and plastic toys were displayed on shelves or under glass in half empty cases. There was a store full of knock-off electronics and tiny washing machines. All of it was bathed in late-afternoon shadow, the lights kept Save or Die low. Locals clutching creased ration books lined up out the door at an egg dispensary.

We came upon a nook where a young woman was selling ice cream bars. A small sign read "$3.00." I asked for one and handed her three CUC $1 coins, realizing even as I dropped them in her hand that the sign was surely referring to nonconvertible CUPs. She whisked the coins away into a cubbyhole below the counter, trying hard to seem merely efficient. She handed me an ice cream on a stick and fixed me with a blank stare. I held her gaze for a yawning moment, not sure what I was waiting for. We were colonizer and colonized, deep in the fuzzy grey market of the tourist economy, wondering who would blink first. "*Gracias*," I said finally, and we walked on down the street.

A few blocks farther along, I came to understand just how much I'd overpaid. The ice cream had been chalky and flavourless and we were still peckish, so we stopped at a corner where an old woman was selling roasted peanuts wrapped in paper cones. I gestured for one and handed her a twenty-five-centavo coin, a twelfth of what I'd paid for the ice cream. She was aghast. An old man standing next to her made an exaggerated goggleeyed gesture of shock and then scooped up as many of the cones as his two hands could hold, nearly everything on her tray. Eventually, we settled on two cones for the quarter, for which she thanked us extravagantly.

I'd handed the girl at the ice cream stall a windfall. She sold lousy ice cream to locals from a stall on the state store shopping street in a largely tourist-free city. (Unlike Havana, which draws hordes of visitors on its own and many more on day trips from nearby Varadero's crowded resort strip, Santiago is too remote for the package tour masses, three hours by road from the much smaller cluster of beach developments near Holguin.) She had no expectation of returning home that night with CUCs in her pocket—a week's wage in a single, accidental hard-currency tip. But we were, after all, Canadians on the sunny end of thousand dollar flights, and what did a couple of misspent CUCs matter here or there? The price of almost everything was arbitrary in Cuba. Normal rules didn't apply. That was part of the fun.

We spent a week in Santiago, and only twice did we encounter anything like a posted exchange rate, both times at live music venues near the main square. The first was at the government-run Artex music store, which sells an exhaustive range of Cuban music CDs (after rum and cigars, probably Cuba's most popular souvenir and its most widely adored cultural export). A small courtyard out the back features live music all afternoon and evening, and a sign at the top of the stairs leading down to the patio lists the admission prices in both convertible and nonconvertible pesos: "CUC $1.00/ CUP $20.00." Up the street at Casa de la Trova, the most storied music hall in Santiago if not all of Cuba, locals were paying CUP $25 for an admission ticket marked "CUC $1.00."

Once, walking past a ration store, I saw rice listed on the chalkboard above the long, weathered wooden counter at $0.25 per pound (CUP, of course). At Patio de Artex's twenty-to-one exchange rate, I'd paid CUP $60—enough to buy 240 pounds of rice—for one barely edible ice cream bar. We could have bought 160 pounds of rice for what we spent to watch an hour of music one fine afternoon on the patio.

Let's talk about that Patio de Artex show. It points to the most obvious reason, beyond the availability and convenience of cheap flights or the historical friendship or the incomparable quality of a real hand-rolled Cohiba, that more than a million Canadians visit Cuba every year (compared, for example, with the 754,000 who travel to the Dominican Republic, where prices are lower, the cigars and rum are equally plentiful, and the logistics are uncomplicated by Communist bureaucracy and the grim exigencies of the Special Period). It's related to why it's no accident that Cuba alone has managed to pass half a century in open, hostile defiance of the world's most powerful nation just to the north. Every country has its character and customs and quirks, but there's a depth of soul to Cuba that puts it in a class by itself. Cuban music has set the tone and the rhythm for much of Latin American music for generations, and it's the most visceral manifestation of the island's indomitable spirit.

So, yes, let's talk about the Patio de Artex show. At the precipitous cliff's edge of the Special Period, even after many grinding months of Save or Die austerity, you can still find a table at Patio de Artex on any old Friday afternoon and watch eight guys in donated T-shirts and Chinese jeans transform a courtyard into one of the best places on earth from which to launch a weekend. Mojitos sweating through plastic cups on the table, the trumpet player muting his horn with his hand to add a vampish growl to the *son* they're tearing up, a propulsion in the rhythm that hauls even a hopeless, doubly left footed non-dancer like me to his feet—this is what you get for your 160-pounds-of-rice admission at Patio de Artex. You get escape, transcendence. The show would have been a bargain at CUC $10 a head.

This is why Canadians come back again and again. And why, perhaps, they bring even more T-shirts and towels and acetaminophen the next time: because these people deserve more for their labour. They deserve better. Yes, this is true of any picturesque beach destination in the impoverished tropics, but in Cuba it's somehow more undeniable. Maybe it's the grinding workaday cruelty of the Special Period, the utter absurdity of America's ongoing embargo. Maybe we delude ourselves, in Mexico or

Jamaica, with the notion that the society's nominal freedom means no absolute barrier exists between our decadent days by the pool and the women slaving away at the messes in our hotel rooms. Anyway, there's something about Cuba that brings the arbitrary nature of wealth and power and material comfort into especially high relief. And so we bring stuff. Gifts. Offerings. Talismans of apology and absolution.

Live music is not hard to find in Santiago de Cuba. The city prides itself on being the place where African rhythms first mated with Spanish harmonies and instrumentation to produce the itinerant nineteenth-century musical tradition called *trova*, the wellspring of Cuba's world-conquering musical culture.

One evening at Casa de la Trova, we caught a fantastic seven-piece group called Ecos del Tivoli who performed in matching suits. At other shows, we heard "Chan Chan," the Buena Vista Social Club's signature tune, played about a dozen different ways. We went to the *paladar* closest to our hotel early one night, and they opened up just for us, and before they even took our orders a kindly older man in a fedora showed up with a guitar to serenade us (his yearning take on "House of the Rising Sun" was a highlight). We bought one of his *son* band's CDs (CUC $10, counting a tip for the serenade) and then saw him in the crowd a couple of nights later at Casa de la Trova, where he cajoled a prostitute into showing me a couple of moves on the dance floor.

One afternoon, as we wandered the back streets around the original Bacardi rum distillery, an old woman approached us on the corner. She explained that she worked in economics and computers but her lifelong passion was opera, and then she asked if we'd like to hear a song. As locals strolled past with little more than a glance—just another afternoon in Santiago—she treated us to a passionate mambo in a voice that revealed years of classical training.

On Calle Heredia, a side street near Santiago's main square, there is a small tourist market. Sidewalk vendors hawk handicrafts, and behind them small shops and kiosks trade in antiques, art, and souvenirs. I repeatedly visited one in particular, a place the size of a walk-in closet stuffed to the rafters with books, postcards, and old Cuban LPs. As soon as I expressed an interest in the records, the shop's proprietor, a genial senior citizen in a newsboy cap, grinned at me around his cigar stub and started yanking out records and throwing them on his phonograph. He tangoed around his shop, pouring out coffees for both of us. I bought priceless *son* records for a CUC or two apiece, and a small stack of '70s back issues of *Bohemia*—once one of Latin America's most important magazines—for the same unit price. For reasons I never fully understood, the old gent threw in a freebie, a foldout postcard packet dated 1958, featuring photos of the La Seo Cathedral in Saragossa, Spain.

What would you consider a fair price for admission to one of the best musical theme parks on earth? Twenty bucks? Fifty? What do they charge to get into the Grand Ole Opry in Nashville? If they'd asked me, as we boarded our flight home, for CUC $10 for the old lady's street corner bolero, I'd have paid it gladly. What I felt most acutely, weeks later, is that I'd failed repeatedly to leave an adequate tip.

Let's talk about where to eat in Santiago (and how to undertip there). The state-run restaurants—the CUC joints for tourists, as well as the CUP places for locals—are a complete waste of time.

The food in the family-run restaurants, the *paladares*, is in another league entirely. *Paladares* were black market operations, just a couple of tables in someone's family kitchen, until the mid-'90s, when some of them were licensed and subjected to byzantine regulations and steep fees. The unlicensed ones, though, remain the best, and we found one around the corner from another *trova* hall, the Casa de las Tradiciones, simply by asking the guy at the door if he knew of a place nearby to eat.

He led us briskly up a side street, where seemingly every twenty something male in the neighbourhood was gathered around a boisterous roadside domino game. As we approached, a young man stepped away from the crowd and introduced himself as Luis. He led us a couple of blocks farther along to a tiny bungalow and invited us to take a seat in the living room, where a woman who appeared to be his grandmother was watching telenovelas. Luis disappeared into a back room for what felt like half an hour. When he finally returned, he ushered us past the kitchen, through a narrow bedroom with kids' bunk beds against one wall, and down a concrete staircase to a small patio. A single table had been set immaculately before a panoramic view of Santiago Bay. *Trova* played on a portable stereo while our host, with a veteran tour guide's ease, rattled off historical details about Santiago's port and its slave trading history.

We noticed a small shrine on the corner of the patio, a wooden box standing on its end, the open side facing outward, with dolls, a bowl of coins, and an egg on a tray arranged inside. There was a cigar and a small wooden cross on top, and a chalk circle drawn on the concrete in front of it, around markings of arrows and skulls. Luis explained that he practised a syncretic faith called

Palo Monte, a common Afro-Cuban religion similar to Santeria. We mentioned that it was the only shrine we'd seen. Everyone has them, he replied, but he didn't bother hiding his. He gave us a business card with the name and address of the *paladar*, the only one of those we saw as well. Amid Cuba's current evolution, Luis was more concerned with positioning his modest business for the next phase than with keeping it from the authorities in the last days of this one.

"In Cuba," he told us, "today is today. *A hoy es hoy. Mañana* is another time."

He served us a variation on the mojito, using basil leaves instead of mint. He called it an *alto del mar*—"above the sea," also the name of his *paladar*—and it was the best drink I had in Cuba. Dinner was whole fried fish garnished with the only red pepper we saw in Santiago, and a delicate creole sauce that was several steps above the licensed *paladares'* offerings in its refinement. When I asked for the bill, he brought me a scrap of paper with "$14.00" written on it. I gave him CUC $20, under-tipping for one of the most memorable meals I've eaten anywhere.

Luis's place was just a couple of blocks from the Museum of the Clandestine Struggle, which we visited a few days later. It was a shrine of another sort, its glass cases containing carefully preserved bloodstained suits and Molotov cocktails from the guerilla street war fought block by block in Santiago for years ahead of Fidel's return from exile, testimony to the long-standing Santiagueran tradition of defiance.

Outside, we stopped to watch three teenagers playing an impromptu stickball game in the street. They had a broom handle for a bat, and they were hammering some kind of makeshift ball off the surrounding buildings with such authority it took a while to realize it wasn't even round. It was an empty pill bottle. I had a sudden, sick flashback to our visit to the Wal-Mart in Antigonish and the "baseballs" entry on my shopping list. I'd searched the sporting goods section for baseballs, but in December in Nova Scotia there weren't any. I'd had a sleeve of tennis balls in my hand at one point but had put them back. With a staggering lack of perspective, guided by some deranged sense of propriety, I'd thought to myself that Cubans were world-class ballplayers who surely honed their batting skills using a properly weighted baseball. Now, though, it was the grandest of my under-tips: the one not given.

The Brisas Sierra Mar is a slightly dishevelled three-star resort sixty-five kilometres down the coast from Santiago, a drive that takes nearly three hours along the craziest lunar-landscaped road I've ever encountered. The hotel is a standard-issue all-inclusive: a pool with a swim-up bar, a few restaurants and lounges, an open-air amphitheatre for nightly cultural shows, a dive shop, a beach that was really something before Hurricane Dennis reduced it to a thin strip of sand in 2005. The clientele was at least three-quarters Canadian when we arrived, a significant number of them repeat visitors who came yearly or even more often, and they lent the place a friendly summer camp vibe. The package tour operators near the front desk all kept binders full of details on excursions, and every one of them described a Cuba beyond the gates where dangerous con artists lurked on every corner; the binders all warned against any unaccompanied travel whatsoever outside the resort.

We had come to Brisas Sierra Mar to dive. The divemaster was a soft-spoken, sharp-witted family man named Edgar. We were the only divers who'd never visited the resort before, and everyone else on our excursion asked after his family. His daughters had been sick, he said, with a pointed shrug that suggested illness could go further south in Cuba than you really wanted to talk about.

Cuba's coral reefs are currently rife with lionfish, stunning creatures with brilliant black and orange stripes and a broad mane of poisonous antennae protruding from their fins. Native to the South Pacific, they are an invasive species in the Caribbean that feasts on defenceless hatchlings up and down the reefs. Edgar brought a speargun on most dives to take out as many as he could, and so one of the great spectator sports was watching the divemaster hunt lionfish. One day, he filleted a few of them back at the dive shop, expertly slicing away the venom-tipped fins using a pair of spears as an Asian cook wields chopsticks. The chef at the beachfront restaurant breaded and deep-fried the fillets for us and served them with fries: lionfish and chips, easily the most memorable meal at the Brisas during our stay.

The morning we left, I headed down to the dive shop with a plastic shopping bag stuffed with gifts for Edgar: a big bath towel, a binder and a children's notebook with a tiger on the cover that our daughter had picked out, plus bottles of ibuprofen, Dramamine, and a children's anti-nausea medication called Nauzene. Edgar had called in sick that morning, but the caretaker at the shop said I could leave the bag in his office. I went in, set it down under Edgar's desk, and then hesitated: what if someone else took it? There was no record of it, of course, no way to guarantee Edgar and his sick daughters would get it. I was invested, I realized, in the arbitrary personal connection. I wanted Edgar to know I was looking out for him. This is often the way of gift giving in Cuba—it's not enough to be the colonial master of the exotic treasures, dispensing them with a sovereign's whim. Even in the act of charity, we want tribute. We want to take a little gratitude home with us.

I left the bag in Edgar's office, knowing that whoever wound up with its contents, their value would be immediately understood and cherished. The stuff would be used and reused, used up, exhausted of its value, and then repurposed. An empty econo-sized ibuprofen bottle would, after all, make a serviceable baseball.

I wasn't ready for the condition of Antonio's home. There are more flattering ways to say it, but at the end of the tour in Santiago when he invited us back, it was so much worse than I expected. I was imagining something like the places that lined the streets on our meanderings around the city: tidy concrete bungalows, cramped but homey spaces like Luis' place.

Antonio led us down an alleyway in a densely populated neighbourhood near the photo studio. There were jumbles of concrete piled atop one another in behind the homes you could see from the street, places filigreed with rusted rebar and roofed in salvaged tin. Antonio lived with his young wife in one of them, which was stacked on top of the slightly larger concrete slab where his mother and sister lived. The entry was up a rickety flight of repurposed wooden stairs. There were two rooms: a front living area with a sink in one corner piled with dirty dishes, and a larger back room with a mattress on the floor. There was a Chinese boom box in the front room with one of those outsize, blinking blue-green displays, and a poster of a Dutch league soccer team tacked to the wall above it. It was a makeshift place, a slum dwelling.

Antonio had had his friend drive us all over town in an ancient Soviet-made automobile mostly held together by force of will.

We'd passed grand colonial mansions—"the houses of the people in Miami," Antonio explained—that now housed educational facilities and cultural centres. He'd taken us to an Afro-Cuban cultural centre and museum that we'd never have found otherwise. On the way to the Spanish fort outside town, we'd pulled off the road and waited while he ran to the stoop of a bungalow to procure two bottles of rum with legendary Matusalem labels. No one has made rum under the name of Matusalem in Santiago since Fidel nationalized the distillery, but it was premium stuff for the discount price of CUC $10 per bottle. He'd known just the right restaurant, an unsanctioned *paladar* that turned out delectable grilled lobster. Throughout, Antonio was personable, forthcoming, full of information and generous with it. He was bilingual, literate, and quick witted. His needs were obvious, unmistakable.

I forgot all that. That he was achingly poor, and I impossibly rich. That his madly uncertain future was riding on how many CUCs he had when the Special Period's precarious economic dance stopped and rendered them as worthless as Ostmarks. In the instant he took the ten-peso note from my hand, I was simply a colonial officer standing before him, momentarily indignant. There had been gifts, and there would be more, and how dare he presume to decide when and where and how they were to be bestowed?

That's the real value of ten convertible pesos: under the right circumstances, it will show you exactly who you are in Cuba. You might not like what you see, but it's still well worth the price.

The day before we left Cuba, we took a taxi to Gibara. Before the Spanish colonists built the country's first railroad and placed its terminus in Santiago, the smaller city had been a major port for the sugar trade. Nowadays, it is a sleepy warren of dilapidated colonial mansions fronting on a gorgeous, breezy stretch of Caribbean Sea. While it's less than an hour's drive from the international airport in Holguin—closer, actually, than the strip of all-inclusive resorts farther down the coast—it sees only the occasional handful of day trippers on excursions. The locals are friendly, the accommodations at private guest houses in those ancient mansions charming if not quite grand, the seafood abundant and delicious. It's a breezy, laid-back, disintegrating dream of a place. Gibara is, in other words, the quintessential off-the-beaten-track hideaway, the sort of place Lonely Planet built a guidebook empire discovering.

We adored Gibara. For CUC $10 each per night, we had a comfortable room in a high-ceilinged colonial townhouse with a broad, quiet, hammock-strung courtyard in back. Within a couple of hours of our arrival, we'd already begun speculating on how cheap and easy it would be to hop a winter charter to Holguin and spend a month there living on next to nothing.

At sunset, we wandered down to the harbour to watch a ferry arrive. It disgorged a steady stream of locals in work clothes on foot, and I'd just begun to wonder if they were employees at the resorts up the coast when my wife, who was taking pictures, slipped off the edge of the curb and twisted her ankle. A crowd soon gathered around us, the faces charged with real concern. Everyone said we should go to the hospital, and someone offered to find us a ride. My wife insisted she was fine; she just needed to rest a minute.

"You're hurt," someone said. "Look at your ankle. Why not go? "

"We're Canadian," my wife answered.

"It's for everyone. Just go."

Cuba has one of the best health care systems in the developing world. Its medical schools train doctors from across Latin America and beyond, and it sends its skilled health professionals all over the globe. Cubans are, as we learned in an instant, offhandedly but beamingly proud of their hospitals. I can't think of anywhere else I've been where the default response to an ankle twist was to go immediately to the hospital.

So we went. It was full dark by the time we arrived. The halls were sporadically under-lit by naked bulbs and fluorescent tubes, the walls and furniture crumbling. We were directed to a waiting area, and my wife was seen ten minutes later by a pair of attentive young doctors, who wrapped her ankle and advised her on care. No one asked us for money or anything else. We were back at our guest house half an hour after we'd left.

This is how Cubans are with what little they have, the things that might be of use to us. Take it, as much as you need. Don't hesitate, don't be shy. Just go.

After my wife was settled in bed, I returned to the hospital. I had a bag with me, our final gift to the Cuban people. My Spanish was so weak and disjointed, the people in the entry hall thought I was a bit unhinged at first, but once I showed them what I had in the bag they found a doctor upstairs to sit with me and register the donation. One large bottle of acetaminophen. The six remaining pills in a blister pack of a dozen decongestants. One bottle of gas relief drops for infants. Two-thirds of a twenty-pack of ballpoint pens. Everything we had left. The least we could give a hospital that offers aid to anyone who shows up on its doorstep but can't reliably purchase its own medication.

The next time we go to Cuba, we'll bring much more, and I'll remind myself to tip better. I've decided on a CUC $10 minimum. It's only fair.

Beyond War and Peacekeeping

Jennifer Welsh

On December 30, 1941, as part of his wartime visit to Canada, British prime minister Winston Churchill addressed an extraordinary joint session of the Senate and House of Commons in Ottawa to thank our country for its steadfast commitment to the Allied cause—through troops, equipment, food and finance, and through its indispensable Empire training scheme for pilots from across the Commonwealth.

Churchill's purpose, however, went beyond expressions of gratitude. His task was also to prepare Canadians for the gruelling months ahead in the fight against Nazi Germany (and, due to the attack on Pearl Harbor earlier that month, Imperial Japan as well). "In a few months, when the invasion season returns," he warned, "the Canadian Army may be engaged in one of the most frightful battles the world has ever seen." In that legendary Churchillian prose, he reminded his listeners of the justness of their cause and the certainty of victory. "There shall be no halting, or half measures, there shall be no compromise, or parley. These gangs of bandits have sought to darken the light of the world; have sought to stand between the common people of all the lands and their march forward into their inheritance. They shall themselves be cast into the pit of death and shame, and only when the earth has been cleansed and purged of their crimes and their villainy shall we turn from the task which they have forced upon us."

According to newspaper accounts of the time, Churchill's words electrified the packed chamber, and consolidated the backing of

Canada's political elite behind his leadership of the war effort. The journalist Margaret Lawrence, a writer for *Saturday Night* magazine, chronicled how a normally dull and grey Commons was transformed by the lights of photographers and movie crews and a powerful microphone to carry Churchill's booming voice—which she described as "a gift from God"—to the whole world. "As the people dispersed and left the Chamber to go their various ways," wrote a reporter for the Ottawa Morning Citizen the next day, "all realized that somehow a strange, indefinable transformation had been worked within their hearts. They weren't quite the same people."[1]

The support for Churchill was matched by a more general embrace of the war effort by the Canadian population. Numerous polls by Gallup and the newly created Canadian Institute of Public Opinion showed in the early months of 1942 a high level of willingness on the part of citizens (both French and English) to accept wartime controls and endure personal sacrifice—including wage and price ceilings, rationing and government control of production in factories. In August 1942, a poll demonstrated that Canadians, both English and French (although the latter less overwhelmingly), opposed any peace deal with Hitler—something Churchill, of course, had tirelessly fought to avoid at all costs.

This was Canada at war. And it is an image that contemporary figures from the Harper government are fond of appealing to. In a speech to the United Nations in September 2011, foreign affairs minister John Baird compared today's critics of Israel, who in his view underestimate the threat from Iran, to the appeasers of fascism prior to the Second World War. Quoting Churchill, he described an appeaser as "one who feeds a crocodile, hoping it will eat him last." Stephen Harper also has a penchant for invoking the "good versus evil" Churchillian mantra, as in an interview with *Maclean's* last July, when he claimed that moral clarity was among the greatest assets one could draw on for foreign policy making. The prime minister went a step further, proclaiming that Canada's history of being on "the right side of important conflicts" had shaped its identity and trajectory as a nation.

CONTESTING THE "WARRIOR NATION"

For an increasingly vocal set of commentators, the tendency of the Harper government to elevate our experience in armed conflict and to depict the world as one marked by danger and epic struggle is part of a broader campaign to transform Canada into a "warrior nation." In a new book with this title, Queen's University historian Ian McKay and writer Jamie Swift contend that determined right-wing forces within the government, academia and the media (including even *Hockey Night in Canada*'s Don Cherry) are endeavouring to fundamentally shift how Canadians think about their country and its history. This "new warrior project" includes efforts to increase military spending, inculcate greater respect for soldiers and "martial values," rebrand Remembrance Day as a celebration of war and instil more muscularity into Canada's foreign policy.

By examining the lives of particular Canadians—including the war veteran turned disarmament advocate Tommy Burns and the Cold War diplomat and founder of the peacekeeping formula Lester Pearson—the authors demonstrate that our country actually has a rich but mixed experience of war, moral crusades and efforts to foster global peace. Indeed, these tendencies have often been mixed within a single figure, as their treatment of Pearson the fierce Cold Warrior (willing to support strong anti-communist measures at home and abroad) and Pearson the peacemaker clearly illustrate. The cardinal sin of the Harperites, McKay and Swift argue in *Warrior Nation: Rebranding Canada in an Age of Anxiety*, is that they honour and promote only one part of that national story—the tale of Canada defending and promoting western, imperialist values by putting its "boots on the ground."

Not surprisingly, peacekeeping is a key aspect of Canada's past that McKay and Swift wish to salvage from the clutches of those peddling the new warrior project. Noah Richler, in another new Canadian book, *What We Talk About When We Talk About War*, constructs a similar defence of peacekeeping against its depiction by right-wing historians, politicians and journalists as "a moniker of political futility, dysfunction of the UN and the misapplication of the strengths, resources and precious lives of the Canadian Forces." The war in Afghanistan, he argues, presented a golden opportunity for the disgruntled opponents of peacekeeping—and its hold on the Canadian imagination—to reorient the Armed Forces toward their "core business" and remind our country's allies that Canada was not averse to the rough and tumble of combat. The success of that venture, of course, has not been so clear-cut.

Like McKay and Swift, Richler bristles at the notion that war fighting has been the defining experience of the Canadian nation. "The claim that the country's borders, its francophone-anglophone duality and its relationships with the United States and abroad were shaped either by wars forced upon it, or by other conflicts that it chose to take part in," he writes, "is the fantasy of a political lobby that, unchecked over the course of the last decade, has seen the country's ability to fight wars as the truest indicator of its maturity." Instead, Richler suggests, it has been resolution of conflict through dialogue and compromise—and not the use of force—that more faithfully reflects the essence of the "Canadian way."

Both of these books are bound to stir up controversy in the months ahead. Their central mission—to wake up Canadians to the ongoing project to militarize their history before their country is changed beyond recognition—will no doubt find a captive audience among those who are both opposed to and inherently suspicious of the Harper majority government. Of the two works, McKay and Swift's seems the more substantive, as it digs more deeply into the historical record and draws more convincingly on deep connections with military figures and families in Kingston, Ontario. But in both cases, many readers will suspect that the scale of the right-wing plot is overblown.

While I am persuaded that there is a clear intent to change both the tenor and substance of Canadian military history and contemporary foreign policy—and I do not much like it either—the Harperites are given rather too much credit in terms of the success of their efforts to rebrand Canada as a warrior nation. Moreover, there are real questions to be asked about the sustainability of such a project. For some inconvenient data, one need only consult the 2012 Harper budget, which illustrates that the regular rises in defence spending that have occurred over the past five years are at an end. It is not just a case of reducing spending increases, but concretely scaling back: by 2014–15, $1.1 billion (or five percent) will be cut from the defence budget and equipment purchases in the range of $3.5 billion will be delayed.[2]

SEEING THE BIGGER PICTURE

These are the details that will no doubt be bandied about in the responses both to Richler and to McKay and Swift. My broader argument, however, is that this particular, and I daresay narrow, debate about militarization under Harper is an unhelpful distraction from a much more important story about the profound changes that have taken place in the nature of armed conflict. It is this transformation, and its implications for Canada, that should be the focus of our attention.

We have seen the effects of this kind of distraction before. Think back, for example, to the hand-wringing over whether or not Canada was still "America's best friend" after distancing itself from the United States during the Iraq war. This concern—which was matched by a series of attempts to "make up" for our dissent, including even our involvement in Afghanistan—not only misconstrued the nature of our relationship with the U.S. (which has withstood many bumps in the road) but diverted our gaze from the seismic shifts in the global distribution of power, which have generated the comparative rise of states such as China and India. Our myopia about the United States left us ill prepared to deal with the opportunities and challenges that such a recalibration of power represent.

HUMAN RIGHTS AND ARMED CONFLICT

Of the many transformations that have occurred in the causes and conduct of armed conflict, including those wrought by revolutions in technology, two stand out.

The first can be broadly described as the increasing prominence of the individual, rather than the sovereign state, in the practice and law of armed conflict. This trend, which is both linked to and fuelled by parallel developments in human rights, has had three principal effects.

First and foremost, it has made the individual one of the central reasons for going to war. So whereas conflicts in previous centuries were about the gain of territory or resources, or defence against attack, many contemporary conflicts have as one of their central purposes the protection of individuals' physical security. The action led by the North Atlantic Treaty Organization (NATO) in Libya last year is the culmination of this trend.

Second, the individual has become an accountable agent for certain criminal acts undertaken during the course of war (whether at the level of commander or soldier), as witnessed by the recent extraordinary trial of former Liberian president Charles Taylor, accused of sponsoring atrocities in neighbouring Sierra Leone.

And third, the centrality of the individual means that international humanitarian law—the law applicable in wartime—is no longer purely a body of reciprocal legal rules agreed to by sovereign states to limit their conduct during war, in order to minimize the suffering of innocents. Instead, those who become embroiled in armed conflict are still seen to possess their core human rights, regardless of what the warring parties believe they need to do out of "military necessity."[3] This has spurred a variety of path-breaking legal challenges by individuals against the actions of military establishments, such as the 2007 Al-Jedda case in the United Kingdom, where a dual Iraqi/British national protested against his detention by British forces in Iraq.

Realists will no doubt retort that these shifts are peripheral, and do not constrain states from pursuing—if necessary, by force—their core national interests. But this assertion is not matched by the concrete steps being taken by many military organizations—for example through changes to training and doctrine and efforts to both count and report civilian deaths—to come to grips with the impact of human rights on the causes and conduct of war.

If the elevation of the individual (and his or her rights) has transformed war, so too has it transformed the practice of peacekeeping. Beginning with the conflict in Sierra Leone in 1999, the UN Security Council now routinely includes civilian protection in peacekeeping mandates, calling on UN contingents to stand up for extreme violations of human rights. Thus, as Canadian scholar Emily Paddon has shown, while during the Cold War–era peacekeepers practised a more passive kind of impartiality, concerned primarily with treating all parties to a conflict in an equal manner, contemporary peacekeepers are expected and mandated to be more assertive, by "penalizing infractions" (as the 2008 *United Nations Peacekeeping Operations: Principles and Guidelines* puts it) against the peace process or broader international norms and principles.[4]

This trend, it seems to me, raises some difficult issues for those such as Richler, who on the one hand want to claim that the essence of the Canadian way is a commitment to human rights, support for international projects such as the International Criminal Court, and strong backing of multilateral organizations such as the United Nations—yet who also long for a supposedly golden era of neutrality. To begin, there is the technical point that peacekeeping has never been about neutrality, which entails standing aside from engaging in political activity; rather, the UN has always described its actions as impartial—a principle that entails positive duties to act without bias toward any party.

But more importantly, when Richler describes peacekeeping (or his preferred catch-all term, "peace operations") as centred on negotiation and nation building, he forgets not only that very particular, liberal values inspire those activities, but also that the "just peace" (his words) he seeks to promote globally is based on a contestable view of justice. So while he may be right in saying that peacekeeping, even in its more muscular form, is not synonymous with war (despite the wish of some Harperites to make it so), it does implicate peacekeepers in activities beyond "tempering" and "adjudicating."

This is not to say that peacekeeping in the traditional sense, as literally keeping warring factions apart through the creation and monitoring of a buffer zone, will never again be relevant. In fact, as I write, international policy makers are wondering whether such an operation might be mounted to keep Sudan and the newly created South Sudan from a devastating and self-defeating military confrontation. Instead, it is to recognize that in many of the UN's more recent peacekeeping efforts, the meaning of impartiality has been stretched almost to the breaking point. This can be demonstrated, for example, by the UN's military strikes against hardware close to the palace of Laurent Gbagbo, the former president of the Ivory Coast, following the stand-off over elections in 2011—an act seen by some as decidedly partial. If the protection of individual civilians has become an explicit goal, then it is difficult to treat all sides as equal.

To understand this dilemma more fully, consider the challenges that civilian protection created for the UN's largest and most expensive peacekeeping mission in the Democratic Republic of the Congo (MONUC, which operated from 1999 to 2010). On the one hand, the robust mandate (which by 2008 had come to include forty-one different peacekeeping tasks) raised expectations within the population that the UN would save them from violence. So when the people of Bukavu were raped and massacred in 2004, and MONUC stood by, violent anti-UN protests ensued. On the other hand, since peacekeeping forces operate in a state on the basis of that state's consent, action that is viewed as violating impartiality can jeopardize the UN's relationship with the host government—as it did when MONUC began to criticize the Congolese government's military action against rebel factions and was subsequently asked by President Joseph Kabila to leave the DRC.

As a result, the consensus on the legitimacy of what Paddon calls "assertive impartiality" is extremely fragile, due to a deep discomfort among some states about the ambitiousness and normative dimensions of recent UN mandates. The March 2011 action against Libya (although not a peacekeeping operation) has heightened the concerns of those states that remain wedded to the norms that underpinned the more passive, Cold War United Nations—namely, self-determination and non-intervention. For those who support the continuation of multilateral approaches to managing international peace and security, understanding and addressing the tensions within the contemporary practice of peacekeeping is a vital task.

THE END OF WAR AS WE KNOW IT?

The second transformation poses a much more serious challenge to those on both sides of the warrior nation divide, for it suggests that our very subject matter here—formal armed conflict—is becoming a relic of the past. If we need to be honest and rigorous about Canada's past and present wars, we should be equally rigorous in analyzing the bigger picture in which our country's particular experience is embedded.

Researchers have noted for at least twenty years the dramatic decline in the incidence of international armed conflict (such as conflict between two states). So, for example, while in 1950 there was an average of six international conflicts per year, there is currently less than one. The reasons for this shift are hotly debated, with some, like Steven Pinker, emphasizing the impact of norms, institutions and changes in values, and others the effect of deterrence (whether through conventional or nuclear arms).[5] Nevertheless, even dyed-in-the-wool realists, who stress the need for states to prepare for the ever-present possibility of armed attack, have been forced to admit that something pretty interesting is going on here.

But what is truly striking about more recent data sets is that they point to the decline and severity in all types of conflict, including civil war.[6] This latter finding challenges the narrative of the first decade of the post-Cold War period, which predicted that "new wars," driven by ethnic hatred, would constitute the policy dilemma of the 21st century.[7] While eighty-one internal armed conflicts occurred in the 1990s, there were only thirty-nine in the following decade. Moreover, those civil wars that did occur—despite the horrific images on our television screens—were less severe, for both civilians and combatants, than those of previous periods.

These figures suggest that Prime Minister Harper's mental map—of a long-term and epic struggle against terrorists and rogue states like Iran—may be the product of a common ailment:

the tendency to idealize the past and exaggerate the dangers of the present. They also highlight that treatises about how to make or keep or build peace are focusing on a kind of conflict (in this case, usually civil war) that—while undoubtedly devastating for those it affects, both directly and indirectly—may be an increasingly rare occurrence.

But although we are seeing a decline in international and civil wars, as they are legally understood, there is a new category of "generalized violence" that is hidden by these formal categories. According to a 2011 report titled *The Global Burden of Armed Violence*, while on average just over half a million people now die annually in violent circumstances, just ten percent of those die in formal conflict settings. Instead, the growing phenomenon of generalized violence accounts for the lion's share of violent deaths around the world, and is concentrated in a relatively small number of countries, such as El Salvador, Jamaica, Colombia, Guatemala and Mexico (Canada's partner in the North American Free Trade Agreement).

These countries do not tend to feature in many discussions about the future role of the Canadian armed forces, or our broader foreign policy. Yet they all experience widespread, large-scale and indiscriminate violence—whether through the systematic repression of their government or their government's failure to effectively address drug, gang or political violence.

Such societies provide a reality check for those who assume that the decline in the incidence of war means we can all "go back to our barracks." Surely these situations call out for some kind of response, if the United Nations is now about protection. And if Richler is right, that the essence of the "Canadian way" is what he calls our "humanitarian internationalist tendencies," then surely we should have something to contribute to these tragedies—many of which are in our own hemisphere.

It has been said that generals too often "fight the last war." That might be true, too, of those who write about and analyze war. If Canadians want to adapt to the changing nature of war, they first need to guard against simplified dichotomies—war versus peace or conflict versus crime—and recognize that today's armed violence has multiple and overlapping motives, and that different types of violence can exist and interact in the same setting.

The next step is to think in more creative, even radical ways about the different entry points that national, regional and international actors might have to both prevent and address today's most dangerous environments. The tragic situations in Guatemala, or Mexico's Ciudad Juarez, require policies that directly address perpetrators and their particular economic motives (such as poverty and unemployment), the means they have to commit violent acts (such as the flow of cheap arms) and the wider institutional setting that permits violence to occur with impunity (such as weak adherence to the rule of law). In the case of Guatemala, for example, the role of the UN has not involved peacekeepers, but rather—through a novel agreement with the national government—assistance in investigating crimes and instances of violence, and efforts to strengthen Guatemalan institutions (such as the Public Prosecutor's Office, civilian police, and national courts) that are confronting illegal groups.[8]

This is a very different agenda for promoting international security than either buying more F-35s (a central plank in Harper's vision for the Canadian military) or creating a new, dedicated peace operations regiment (an idea proposed by Richler). Indeed, it is an agenda that may not engage military actors much at all.

This does not mean that national armed forces, to safeguard our sovereignty and security, are a relic of the past. But it does mean that we need to talk not only about Canada's history of war, and the mistakes of current wars such as Afghanistan, but also of what war is likely to look like for our children and grandchildren.

ENDNOTES

[1] For more on Churchill's visit and speech, see David Dilks' *The Great Dominion: Winston Churchill in Canada, 1900-1954.* (G7 Books, 2005).

[2] It should be noted that the controversial plans to buy new F35s do not figure into the budget figures. This purchase will still go ahead but will not show up on the books until 2016.

[3] For more on this transformation, and the particular relationship between human rights and armed conflict, see Ruti Teitel's *Humanity's Law* (Oxford UP, 2011).

[4] For further discussions on the tensions inherent in contemporary peace-keeping, see Emily Paddon's "Partnering for Peace: Implications and Dilemmas" in *International Peacekeeping* Vol. 18.5.

[5] For a comprehensive treatment of the data, see Steven Pinker's *The Better Angels of Our Nature: the Decline of Violence in History and Its Causes* (Allen Lane, 2011).

[6] The main sources consulted for this piece are the Uppsala Data Conflict Program, available at www.pcr.uu.se//researchucdp; the 2009-10 *Human Security Report*, available at www.hsrgroup.org; and *The Global Burden of Armed Violence 2011*, available at www.genevadeclaration.org.

[7] This thesis was most clearly expressed in Mary Caldor's *New and Old Wars: Organized Violence in a Global Era* (Polity, 2006).

[8] The agreement, signed in late 2006, created the International Commission against Impunity in Guatemala.

Author Bios

DENISE BALKISSOON is a freelance journalist in Toronto. She has won a National Magazine Award for her coverage of real estate, and is the co-editor of the race and ethnicity blog *The Ethnic Aisle.*

KAREN CONNELLY is the author of nine books of best-selling non-fiction, fiction, and poetry, the most recent being *Burmese Lessons*, a memoir about her experiences on the Thai-Burma border. She has won the Pat Lowther Award for her poetry, the Governor General's Award for her non-fiction, and Britain's Orange Broadband Prize for New Fiction for her first novel, *The Lizard Cage*. Her other books include *Grace and Poison, One Room in a Castle, This Brighter Prison, The Disorder of Love*, and *The Small Words in My Body*. Married with a young child, she divides her time between a home in rural Greece and a home in Toronto.

GORČIN DIZDAR was born in Sarajevo in 1984. In 2001, he won a Soros Open Society scholarship, enabling him to complete his secondary education at Whitgift School, London, UK. He then completed a B.A. in Philosophy and Modern Languages (German) at Wadham College, Oxford. After two years in Sarajevo, during which he worked in advertising, political analysis and organization of cultural events, he returned to academia, completing an M.A. in Humanities at York University, Toronto where he continues to work towards a PhD. During the summers, he manages the Mak

House, a cultural centre and art gallery in the Bosnian town of Stolac, dedicated to his grandfather, the Bosnian poet Mak Dizdar.

ROBERT FINLEY lives in Newfoundland and Nova Scotia and teaches literature and creative writing at the Memorial University of Newfoundland. He is the author of *The Accidental Indies* (McGill-Queens), a book of lyrical essays, and, with Patrick Friesen, Aislinn Hunter, Anne Simpson and Jan Zwicky, of *A Ragged Pen: Essays on Poetry and Memory* (Gaspereau). Currently he is at work on an ongoing series of video installations in and around the city of Halifax (with François Gaudet); along with a series of essays combining image and text toward a construction of home; and he has just completed a collaborative translation (with Dr. Marta Marìn) from the Catalan of Joaquim Amat-Piniella's 1946 novel of the German camps, *KL Reich*.

ERIC FRIESEN is a broadcaster, writer, speaker and consultant on music, culture and faith. He has spent much of his life as a network classical music and culture host and producer for Minnesota Public Radio (NPR) and CBC Radio, where he hosted such programs as Studio Sparks, In Performance, and Onstage at Glenn Gould Studio, as well as the celebrated documentary series, *The Concerto According to Pinchas, The Concerto According to Manny* and *Peter and the Symphony*. He is currently the Program Director for a new classical and jazz radio station which will launch in Winnipeg in late 2013. He lives with this wife, artist Susan Friesen, on Amherst Island, near Kingston.

SIERRA SKYE GEMMA is an award-winning writer and journalist who presently resides with her husband and son in Vancouver, BC. Her essay "The Wrong Way" won the 2012 Edna Staebler Personal Essay Contest and a 2013 National Magazine Award for Best New Magazine Writer. Currently working towards an MFA in Creative Writing at the University of British Columbia, She also works as an Executive Editor of *PRISM* and co-writes the blog *Regressive Parenting.*

WAYNE GRADY was born in Windsor, Ontario, in 1948. He has written fifteen books, including works of science and nature as *The Bone Museum, Bringing Back the Dodo, The Quiet Limit of the World,* and *The Great Lakes,* which won a National Outdoor Book Award in the U.S. With his wife, novelist Merilyn Simonds, he co-authored *Breakfast at the Exit Café: Travels Through America.* And with David Suzuki he co-wrote the international bestseller *Tree: A Life Story.* In 1989, he won the Governor General's Award for his translation of Antonine Maillet's *On the Eighth Day* and his most recent translation is of Louis Hamelin's *October 1970* in 2013. Also in 2013, he published his first novel, Emancipation Day. Grady teaches creative writing in the optional-residency MFA program at the University of British Columbia. He lives with his wife, Merilyn Simonds, in the countryside near Kingston, Ontario.

MICHELLE KAESER is a writer living in Vancouver. Her short stories and essays have appeared in a variety of publications, including *Prairie Fire, Cicada, The Potomac Review, Xtra West,* and *This Magazine,* among others.

MARK KINGWELL has been a Professor of Philosophy at the University of Toronto since 1991 and, since 2001, a contributing editor of *Harper's Magazine*. He is the author or co-author of sixteen books of political, cultural and aesthetic theory, including the national bestsellers *Better Living* (1998), *The World We Want* (2000), *Concrete Reveries* (2008), and *Glenn Gould* (2009). His most recent books are a collection of his essays on art and philosophy, *Opening Gambits* (2008); with Joshua Glenn and cartoonist Seth, *The Idler's Glossary* (2008) and *The Wage Slave's Glossary* (2011); and a collection of his essays on politics and the human imagination, *Unruly Voices* (2012). He has lectured extensively in Canada, the U.S., Europe, the Middle East, and Australia and has held visiting posts at Cambridge University, the University of California at Berkeley, and the City University of New York, where he was the Weissman Distinguished Visiting Professor of Humanities in 2002. He is the recipient of the Spitz Prize in political theory, National Magazine Awards for both essays and columns, a research fellowship at the Jackman Humanities Institute, and in 2000 was awarded an honorary DFA from the Nova Scotia College of Art & Design for contributions to theory and criticism.

KATHERINE LAIDLAW is a writer and editor based in Montreal.

PATRICIA ROBERTSON grew up in British Columbia and received her MA in Creative Writing from Boston University. Her most recent book is *The Goldfish Dancer: Stories and Novellas.* Her first collection of fiction, *City of Orphans*, was shortlisted for the Ethel Wilson Fiction Prize, and her work has also been shortlisted for the Journey Prize, the CBC Literary Awards, the Pushcart Prize, and the National Magazine Awards (three times). In 2014 she will be the first writer-in-residence at the Kingston Frontenac Public Library in Ontario. She lives in Whitehorse, Yukon.

MARYAM SANATI is a writer for a variety of Canadian publications, and is editorial director of special projects for *Toronto Life*. She is the former editor-in-chief of *Chatelaine*, and has held top editorial positions at *The Globe and Mail*, *Report on Business* and *Shift*.

CHRIS TURNER is one of Canada's leading voices on sustainability, livable cities and the global clean-tech boom. His most recent book is *The War on Science: Muzzled Scientists and Wilful Blindness in Stephen Harper's Canada*. He is also the author of *The Leap* and the bestsellers *The Geography of Hope* and *Planet Simpson*. His magazine writing has earned nine National Magazine Awards and appears regularly in *The Walrus*, *The Globe & Mail*, *Alberta Views*, *Canadian Geographic*, and many other national and international publications. He was the Green Party candidate in the 2012 Calgary Centre by-election and a 2013 Berton House writer-in-residence in Dawson City, Yukon. He lives in Calgary with his wife and two children.

JENNIFER M. WELSH is Professor in International Relations at the University of Oxford, co-director of the Oxford Institute for Ethics, Law and Armed Conflict, and a Fellow of Somerville College. In 2013, she was appointed by the UN Secretary General to serve as his Special Adviser on the Responsibility to Protect. She is a former Jean Monnet Fellow of the European University

Institute in Florence, and was a Cadieux Research Fellow in the Policy Planning Staff of the Canadian Department of Foreign Affairs. She has taught international relations at the University of Toronto, McGill University, and the Central European University (Prague), and spent three years as an Associate with McKinsey & Company in Toronto. She has been the Distinguished Visiting Fellow at Massey College (University of Toronto) in 2005, and a 2006 recipient of a Leverhulme Trust Research Fellowship and a Trudeau Fellowship. Welsh has also served as a consultant to the Government of Canada on international policy, and acts as a frequent commentator in Canadian media on foreign policy and international relations. She currently lives in Oxford, England with her husband and two children.

Editors Bios

CHRISTOPHER DODA is a poet, editor and critic living in Toronto. He is the author of two collections of poetry, *Among Ruins* and *Aesthetics Lesson* and is working on a third, a book of glosas based on hard rock and heavy metal lyrics to be titled *Glutton for Punishment*. He is also the book review editor for the online journal *Studio*.

STEPHEN MARCHE is the author of several books of fiction and non-fiction including *Love and the Mess We're In*, *How Shakespeare Changed Everything*, *Shining at the Bottom of the Sea* and *Raymond and Hannah*. His work has frequently appeared in *Esquire* (for which he was a finalist for the ASME National Magazine Award for Commentary), *The New York Times*, *The Wall Street Journal*, *The New Republic*, *Salon.com*, *The Globe and Mail* and *The Toronto Star*.

Permissions for Best Canadian Essays 2013

Grateful acknowledgment is made to the following for permission to reprint previously published material:

"The Bully Mob" appeared in *Toronto Life* (January 2012) copyright 2012 by Denise Balkissoon. Used with permission of author.

"Washing the Body" appeared in *Alberta Views* (November 2012) copyright 2012 by Karen Connelly. Used with permission of author.

"The Graves of the Ancestors" appeared in *Descant* (Issue 156) copyright 2012 by Gorčin Dizdar. Used with permission of author.

"The Approaches" appeared in *Malahat Review* (Issue 180) copyright 2012 by Robert Finley. Used with permission of author.

"A Tangle of Rainbows: A *Quartet* for the End of Time" appeared in *Queen's Quarterly* (Vol 119. 4) copyright 2012 by Eric Friesen. Used with permission of author.

"The Wrong Way" appeared in *New Quarterly* (Issue 124) copyright 2012 by Sierra Skye Gemma. Used with permission of author.

"On the Willing Suspension of Disbelief" appeared in *Event* (Issue 41.1) copyright 2012 by Wayne Grady. Used with permission of author.